VIDEO
The Educational Challenge

Robin Moss

CROOM HELM
London & Canberra

Croom Helm Ltd, Provident House, Burrell Row,
Beckenham, Kent BR3 1AT

British Library Cataloguing in Publication Data

Moss, Robin
    Video
    1. Video tape recorders and recording.
    I. Title
    778.59'9   TK6655.V5
    ISBN 0-7099-1747-3

Printed and bound in Great Britain by
Biddles Ltd, Guildford and King's Lynn

Th:

CONTENTS

For Irene, with my love

ACKNOWLEDGEMENTS

Good ideas travel fast and are widely shared. Those that appear in this book are unlikely to be wholly original and I have tried to attribute credit wherever possible. I *can* claim exclusive responsibility for any errors of judgement or detail that may be found.

My thanks are due to all colleagues and friends at the University of Leeds, with whom I have worked for the past ten years, for their ingenuity and efforts which have constantly reinvigorated my own work. I also owe a debt of gratitude to my many friends in the Educational Television Association, as well as elsewhere in the worlds of broadcasting and education, who remain remarkably patient with me. The manuscript was transformed into typescript with characteristic precision and in record time by Jennifer Dartnall, to whom, as ever, my thanks. At home, my wife Irene, who has a career of her own to pursue, showed skill and generosity in encouraging the work to its completion, as well as commenting sagely on various passages. Our children James and Charlotte also co-operated, despite their feeling that watching television with them would have been a much more sensible activity. In the end our cats really did very little damage, despite their persistent dawn custom of sitting on the manuscript whilst I was actually writing.

Robin Moss,
Oxenhope.

INTRODUCTION

This book was researched during 1981 and 1982 and written in the course of a few weeks in the summer and autumn of 1982. It represents an attempt to describe the present and immediately future role of video in communication and in education. The business of prophecy is a chancy one at the best of times and at this moment it is especially difficult to predict future political and economic trends which obviously have great relevance to the issues under discussion here. In addition, it is for once no exaggeration to call the changes in the technology of video itself 'explosive'. Nevertheless, I was invited to 'draw a map' of the educational territory in which that mysterious beast, video, may be found and I have tried to do so. As I have written, I have become aware of what seem even more significant, albeit more complex subjects. It will be immediately apparent from Chapter 1 what I mean, but it may be as well to clarify my purpose now by outlining the plan of the book and also to define certain terms that will recur.

The three parts of the book discuss three major themes. In Part One, entitled 'Education and Vision', I have been mainly concerned with the story of television in education till now. In Part Two, 'Video, Communication, Education', I have tried to draw the map I was asked to design, describing the role of video at present and in the immediate future, in the communication of information, in the home and in education. Finally, in Part Three, the role of 'Video and New Patterns of Study' is explored. I am conscious that the latter is the most tentative discussion in that the developments covered depend to an extent on many extraneous factors. Still, a major purpose of this book is to draw attention to the particular potential of video in learning at a distance, in more open patterns of study and in continuing education. Briefly, I am convinced — with many others — of the challenge posed to conventional methods of education and even to the content of education itself — by the new society into which we are rapidly moving. Whether education accepts that challenge at once or is forced to do so belatedly, video will play an important part in how it is met. For those who regard education as a delight, something to be enjoyed by all citizens throughout life, the current turmoil and the new prospects are extremely exciting.

Some readers will not have the time or inclination to study the whole book in detail. For their benefit, and to assist reviewers and abstractors, there follows a brief synopsis of each of the ten chapters forming the book. The bibliography and the index are also intended to be useful and will repay active study. I have already been asked why this publication, given its content and purpose, is not available in video format. Such an adaptation would be perfectly imaginable, for this material as for many other texts, and would carry the advantage — if the overall purpose and framework is sound — of permitting ready updating of any part.

Synopsis

Education and Vision

1. Educational Traditions and the Challenge of Video. Plato's view of education as helping everyone to develop their own powers of vision has been overwhelmed by the authoritarian tradition of teaching as the filling of empty vessels. The lecture mode is the method of choice for education, even at university level. Despite clear evidence of the relative inefficiency of the method, students at all levels generally demonstrate great skill in coping with the problems posed. Video, among other new technologies, offers education a challenge to rethink much of its methods and content, helping it tilt the balance away from teacher-centred instruction towards learner-centred study. It also offers the advantage of utilising vision, that powerful but neglected sense, in new ways.

2. Educational Broadcasting. The traditions of educational broadcasting are undergoing radical change at this time, for a variety of reasons. The relative failure of the traditional contribution of broadcast television to education is discussed, as are new approaches that offer some prospect for educational broadcasting's survival, given ingenuity, adaptability and co-operation with other agencies.

3. Educational Television Units. Most British universities and other educational institutions have acquired television production and distribution units in the past decade or so. Their difficulties, both technical and in terms of relationships with teaching staff, have begun to be overcome, and they can look forward to a healthy and indeed expanding role, contributing influentially to internal study packages and to external sales of study materials, if initial conservative reaction in a time of retrenchment can be resisted.

Video, Communication, Education

4. Video and Communication. The effect of microelectronics on our society includes a revolution in television, by technical improvements in the industry itself and by the transformation of television receivers into video display units. The resources of videotex open up a vast range of information to citizens. The arrival of satellite broadcasting together with cable systems implies further important educational and cultural influences for video in the future.

5. Video at Home. The most familiar new role for video lies in the home, where the consumer-led revolution has already made considerable progress. The arrival of the videodisc and similar novel devices implies, together with the convergence of microcomputers with video technology, an educational potential for video in the home and elsewhere that is hard to overestimate, especially as governments are themselves encouraging the process.

6. Video in the School. Children already spend more time watching television than at school. Video can be harnessed to provide valuable support both for the retraining of teachers, urgently required, and for lifeskills training for pupils as traditional approaches to career and work are redefined. The collaborative creation by children of educational video material has already been shown to have considerable benefit in promoting communication and social skills as well as increased motivation and intellectual gains.

7. Video in Further and Higher Education. Educational television units in further and higher education can be expected to play a major part in four likely developments. *Communication* within institutions and with other agencies will require greater reliance on visual material; *interpretation* of the institution's role to the outside world will more often be expressed in visual form than hitherto; *expansion* of its influence will be encouraged by sales and exchange of video materials; *transformation* of teaching methodology will take place gradually, and video will play a key part. In all these burgeoning activities, the changes will be further encouraged as new types of demand are made of education by society.

Video and New Patterns of Study

8. Video in Distance Learning. The achievement of the Open University in the past decade has been widely admired, but the potential of video for distance learning is as yet hardly explored, in Britain or abroad. The growth of video courses for retraining of professional staff in North America and the arrival of the Open Tech learning systems point the way to intriguing developments that should have particularly valuable implications for the Third World.

9. Video in Open Learning. In what way can video play a distinctive part in the promotion of open learning? Video, as distinct from broadcast television (which should have a continued importance in this context), will be able to draw and retain adult learners, unused and probably hostile to conventional adult education methods. It may offer inspiration to a minority because of its ability to represent and stimulate ideas not readily expressed in written form.

10. Continuing Education. Continuing education is a concept that embraces not only retraining in the broadest sense, but the struggle to create a true democracy of the intellect, whereby, as Bronowski put it, 'knowledge sits in the homes and heads of ordinary people with no ambition to control others'. Video can play a part in this campaign, not only, as already stressed, by the accessibility it offers to ideas and information, but also by promoting study skills. The growth of service industries in European economies, as elsewhere, and the decline in traditional manufacturing industries, implies not only a vastly increased need for retraining in countries both north and south of the equator, but the expansion of video-centred creativity for education and training in an international as well as national sense.

*   *   *

Certain words and phrases that recur in the text deserve explicit definition at the outset. For those unfamiliar with basic terms in electronics, the *New Penguin Dictionary of Electronics* provides valuable information and makes entertaining reading (Young, 1979). If you are seeking an introduction to the usage of video equipment in the home, an excellent guide is available in the shape of *The Complete Handbook of Video* (Owen and Dunton, 1982). I have used those texts myself where necessary, and in addition have tried to employ the following terms consistently, with the meanings listed. Several of the definitions are derived from citations made in John Maddison's useful work of reference, *National Education and the Microelectronics Revolution* (Maddison, 1980).

Continuing education. As explained in Chapter 10, although the term is used by some as a synonym for retraining activities, it is generally employed in this book in the wider sense of education throughout life, or the French 'l'education permanente'.

Convergence. The process whereby microprocessor-based information technology and video devices are integrated into unified systems or machines. The terms 'telematics' and 'informatics' are used by some writers to describe such systems and the information they handle.

Distance learning. Study of a body of knowledge or a specific topic in a place physically remote from the institution disseminating the study materials (typically a package or packages of text and/or other materials delivered by mail), so that face-to-face tuition is relatively infrequent.

Educational technology. The Council for Educational Technology for the United Kingdom defines the phrase (see Chapter 1) as referring to the design of learning systems to integrate with teaching techniques to achieve stated ends. UNESCO in 1977 identified (Maddison, 1980, 10) 33 definitions, of which the following (formed *c*. 1974) has endured: 'the systematic application of scientific and technical knowledge to the processes of learning and teaching'.

Educational television. The creation and use of television and video for education and/or training. Organisations linking those who work professionally or who have an academic interest in this field include the Educational Television Association (based in the United Kingdom) and the National Association of Educational Broadcasters (based in the United States).

Microelectronics. Branch of electronics concerned with the realisation of electronic circuits or systems from microminiaturisation of electronic parts, sub-assemblies and assemblies, using photo-reduction techniques. An integrated circuit or microcircuit is a complete circuit manufactured as a single package into or on top of a single chip of silicon. See Chapter 4.

Open learning. See Chapter 9.

Telesoftware. A system whereby programs for a microcomputer (software) are transmitted by teletext directly to a microprocessor within or linked to a television receiver. See Chapter 4.

Television. Telecommunication of visual and aural information by transmission to receivers or by closed-circuit distribution via cable. Where distinguished from video in this book (e.g. in Part One) emphasis is being laid on control of the signals being central rather than with the viewer.

Video. Replay of television material from a recorder or other independently controlled device; material designed for such a purpose. The term is used by others to describe the picture signal from a television camera (e.g. Young, 1979); in popular usage, it encompasses the industries supplying the devices and the television material for playback. In Britain at least, because of the growth of home video usage, the term is particularly associated with domestic recorders or players originally used for entertainment purposes. See Chapter 4.

Videotex. Systems for the dissemination of textual and graphic information by electronic means, under the selective control of the viewer (Maddison, 1980, 12). See Chapter 4 for a discussion of the subsumed terms 'teletext' and 'viewdata'.

Part One

EDUCATION AND VISION

1 EDUCATIONAL TRADITIONS AND THE CHALLENGE OF VIDEO

'Mystery, Mastery and Open Minds' was the title of a public lecture I delivered at Leeds a few years ago (Moss, 1979, 138). My theme was the role of audio-visual media in education and training, and in particular their influence on the development of the educational aim of *mastery* of oneself and one's environment, rather than of mere certification in a particular professional *mystery*. I aligned myself firmly with those who work to open up the educational treasure-house to as many citizens as care to gain access to it, at whatever moments in their lives and however frequently they choose to knock upon this or that educational door. This book explores these ideas in greater detail and maps out paths which those who wish to use video in education and training may be able to follow, in the confusing and revolutionary technological landscape that is predicted for the last 20 years of the twentieth century. In this chapter, a discussion of some of the authoritarian traditions that have structured educational practice over many generations, and their lasting effects on our society's schooling, is followed by a brief discussion of the relative failure to date of educational technology to contribute effectively to education and training. The last part of the chapter will discuss the concept of education and of open learning, as well as the contributions that video can now make to the realisation of both. Later chapters cover these topics in more detail.

Plato, in the seventh book of his *Republic*, defined education as the business of helping each citizen to develop innate powers of vision by turning in the right direction towards the light. He emphatically rejected the concept of education as 'inserting into the mind knowledge that was not there before – as if putting sight into blind men's eyes'. Yet the latter concept has been the longer lived and the dominant one, over the two thousand and more years since this discussion of education, the earliest one of which we have a record. Why? Perhaps because Plato's own model of society itself is authoritarian, so that in a much earlier passage, discussing the influence of literature on education – a very great influence in Greek and Roman society – he quotes approvingly a passage from Homer that paints a very different image from the libertarian one referred to above. Having said that the rulers of society will want their young to be 'self-controlled', Plato goes on (*Republic*, 3,

389) to praise Homer's hero Diomedes for rebuking a grumbling soldier for disobedience. In an earlier passage, Homer describes King Odysseus 'raising a bloody weal on his shoulders with his gold-studded staff' for similar impertinence (*Iliad*, 2, 265): for, as Plato puts it, self-control consists in obedience to one's rulers as well as control of one's own desires. Whether or not we agree with the ethical judgement implicit in such a definition, the implication for educational practice runs quite counter to the idea of assisting citizens to develop their own innate powers of vision: 'self-control', by this definition, implies acceptance of authority, of instruction and of discipline, rather than individual growth and acquisition of understanding by one's own realisation of truths.

The tension between these two aspects of education, which one might try to describe as 'teaching and learning' or, less helpfully, 'training and education', has tended to resolve itself by the claim that the one precedes the other in an ordered educational system. The trained mind, having received basic information, proceeds to burgeon into learning and eventually understanding, perhaps even discovering new knowledge, on its own. Yet there are contradictions apparent in this model as actually experienced in modern society, contradictions which are becoming more manifest at this moment. Primary education, at one end of the spectrum of experience, is nowadays in most societies concerned with exploration, understanding and delight, rather than learning by rote or education. By contrast, study in higher education is still marked by a high proportion of lectures to large groups of students, despite their having by that stage acquired a considerable body of knowledge on their chosen subject and having shown evidence of great ability and of 'a well-trained mind'. The final stages of higher education are marked, at least in the Anglo-Saxon tradition, by small-group and even individual tuition, but it is hardly surprising that many undergraduates find it difficult to make the psychological shift from the disciplined reception of lecture material to the creative endeavours of the tutorial. What about all our *other* citizens? In Britain, the 'age participation rate' (the proportion of all those under 21 who enter full-time higher education) has never yet exceeded 14.2 per cent, so that the vast mass of citizens rarely, if at all, experience these opportunities. The most recent study (Halsey, Heath, Ridge, 1980) of the distribution of these opportunities across social class in 1972 Britain, shows 20 per cent of service-class boys (i.e. professional and managerial parents) entering higher education (with an average IQ of 120.8), compared with less than 2 per cent of working-class boys (average IQ

127.4). The remaining 98 per cent of working-class children are unlikely to have had any significant experience at all of that tutorial-style education which Socrates described as his ideal.

Authority, in the sense of confidence and justification for the expression of a view, has been confused, in the area of education, with its other meaning of the power to impose obedience on inferiors. As we have seen, the tension between the two was manifest in the fourth century before Christ, but it has become more marked in the educational reappraisal which followed the Industrial Revolution. For most citizens in our society, education is far from an enlivening experience. Those who profess admiration of the system's success are either themselves professionally dependent on it for their livelihood, or come from that very small and select group that has reached and passed through the nirvana of higher education with enjoyment. The bulk of our people would probably agree with Sir Walter Scott that 'all men who have turned out worth anything have had the chief hand in their own education'; and a fair proportion of the select group mentioned would also agree. A period of doubt about the contribution of education to society set in, from the early 1970s, for the first time since the eighteenth-century enlightenment. As the Chairman of the Schools' Council for Curriculum and Examination has put it, it is easy to include education in a general loss of faith in the inevitability of progress, but 'the search for an alternative faith is a bitter experience, so far uncompleted' (Tomlinson, 1981, 727).

Doubts have always been expressed about the efficacy of certain traditional teaching methods, yet they continue to hold enormous sway. I remember as an inexperienced teacher approaching my first lesson with 'the early leavers', in a secondary modern school (i.e. low achievement children, predominantly working-class) in a Midlands town. Sensing my trepidation, a much older man advised me to try two strategies that he had found very useful, in case of trouble: 'to read 'em a story, or, if they don't feel like that, write something on the blackboard and get 'em to copy it into their books'. The latter suggestion seemed almost ludicrous, but the group proved to be so well socialised for it that they helpfully proposed it themselves after some brilliant idea of my own had failed once again to ignite the collective imagination. Despair and curiosity drove me, just once, to try the idea. It worked, beautifully: peace returned to the classroom; the children, five weeks from being cast out into the world of work or unemployment, contentedly sucked their pencils and laboriously copied prose they did not even try to understand. The task was familiar, within their competence, involved no thought or energy. What an epitaph upon the educational achievements of our society over the past century, since the Forster Act first brought universal educational opportunities to our people! How far removed was that warm summer day's event (apparently a familiar enough routine for the group) from the magical atmosphere that we claim for our educational institutions! Here are the star-spangled words of one of our great educationists, describing the justification for a university, as quoted by the Chancellor of Sheffield University and former Chairman of the University Grants Committee, Sir Frederick Dainton:

> It preserves the connection between knowledge and the zest of life
> . . . A fact is no longer a bare fact; it is invested with all its possibili-
> ties. It is no longer a burden on the memory: it is energising as the
> poet of our dreams, and as the architect of our purposes. (Whitehead,
> 1951, quoted by Dainton, 1979, 34)

Should the chasm between such exciting, imaginative experiences and the school life of our less able children, be quite so enormous?

Changing tack somewhat, can one be sure that Whitehead's vision of the university in action is what even the bulk of undergraduates actually enjoy? Sir Walter Moberly, who was also Chairman of the UGC a generation earlier than Sir Frederick Dainton, expressed serious doubts about the preferred lecture method, shortly after the Second World War. Sir Walter described the lecture as 'everywhere the chief normal means of instruction', yet he listed five serious criticisms of its predominance, which some were even then attacking as a particularly harmful example of academic inertia and conservatism. The accusations were that lecturing should be far less prevalent, because:

1. Lecturing, as an impersonal form of mass-production, is inappro-priate to university study which aims to promote individual excellence.
2. The students' passive attitude and desperate struggle to take adequate notes prevents proper intellectual exercise.
3. 'The whole performance is incredibly wasteful of time. The number of man-hours consumed is . . . quite disproportionate to the intellectual harvest that is reaped.' Circulation or publication of the lecture text would be much more economical.
4. Students come to assume that lectures will supply all the material they need for a good degree (as suggested by the UGC's own

Report, 1929-35).
5. 'A considerable proportion of lectures are bad.' Little attention has been paid to the technique of lecturing, and 'lecturers seldom improve, for they suffer from an almost total lack of criticism' from their audience, too polite or shy to comment. (Moberly, 1949, 192-5)

These criticisms are, of course, familiar. So are the responses to them, both those that are stated, and the tacit ones. Those who defend the predominance of lecturing claim that the difficulties faced by students in making adequate records are the price that must be paid for the need to 'cover the ground' adequately. The need to lecture so much, it is claimed, continues because of the constantly shifting frontiers of research and the vital necessity to update and review academic statements; conversely, it is claimed that the thunderbolt of inspiration, the last-minute brilliancy, which strikes the lecturer as he drives in to work, is a frequent contribution to a lecture course which in itself justifies the predominance of lecturing. Finally, it is often said that the time consumed is as nothing to the hours that would be wasted if other methods were adopted for instruction, and it is of course nonsense to suggest that any but a very small proportion of lecturers are less than competent. Unspoken are the thoughts that lecturing is actually a relatively easy mode of teaching to perform, and that circulation of texts would lay the lecturer open to criticisms from which he is protected by delivery of a reading. The authority that is conferred on the lecturer by the activity, in some cases an important element in his professional *raison d'être* — the word is, after all, in his title — must also be a factor in the fierce defence of it as a practice. It is also undeniable that the simplicity of the procedure (and indeed the amount of time it consumes) militate against modifying it or replacing it with other methods. If pressed hard, some academics will reply that they themselves survived the experience of attending lectures, so why should not new generations? This not only ignores evidence on the inefficiency of the process but also the fact that by definition academics themselves form a small proportion of the already narrowly selected group that enters higher education; they are not even themselves typical of the range of undergraduates for whom they are responsible.

Lecturing will continue, as a chosen method of teaching, in universities, colleges and schools. As a means of handing on information to a large group of well-motivated and intelligent acolytes, it is relatively swift, well understood by both teacher and taught, and it minimises the demands upon the teacher for preparation of his or her lesson. Research evidence can now tell us a lot about lecturing and note-taking, and illuminates much about the process and definition of education itself. An ingeniously designed handbook by George Brown of Nottingham University summarises 20 years of research findings and suggests a series of exercises and activities to enhance lecturing skills and understanding (Brown, 1978). Successful explanation of novel material is marked by a well-designed structure, its composition underlined to listeners as each key passage begins; it is enlivened by the lecturer's manifest interest in the subject (or in appropriate parts of it) by variations in student activity, and even, as Sydney Smith said of Macaulay's conversation, by 'occasional flashes of silence that are perfectly delightful'. A successful lecture also closes with a summary and a clear end.

References to flashes of silence reminds one that students do not naturally and instinctively comprehend and note down a lecturer's messages (assuming they are delivered in an orderly manner) in an orderly fashion, let alone review, interpret and learn from their notes effectively. Physiological factors inhibit their note-taking efficiency over the traditional one-hour period of a lecture (a marked decline in attention after 20 minutes and a marked peak just before the end has often been measured). Note-taking itself is not efficient: a 1974 estimate based on experiment put the average amount of information noted at 11 per cent of that actually delivered. If no review is undertaken within 24 hours, preferably with further note-taking and amendments to the original copy, at least 60 per cent of a lecture's information content is forgotten, and 80 per cent within a week (Brown, 1978, 44-5 and 101). Given these well-known facts, which any lecturer could replicate by his or her own action at any time, either as teacher or student, it is surprising that little or no assistance is given to the student at the outset of a course. Brown (1978, 100) gives a number of simple hints which are designed to help students take notes in a clear and orderly manner, and to allow for and encourage the vitally important process of note-taking *after* lectures. It is a measure of how far the concept of 'authority' has become synonymous with that of status and power in the context of lecturing, that such a procedure as advising students how to get the best out of attending lectures would be regarded by many lecturers as unnecessary mollycoddling. Yet students on degree courses may attend 400-500 hours of this activity, some of them barely recognising until too late how important their scribbled, disorderly material will become to them just before the examinations. Another set of guidelines for lecturers, based on considerable research, has been published by Hartley and Davies (1978) and the study of student learning by Laurillard (1979) is also relevant: both are discussed in Mantz Yorke's useful source book (Yorke, 1981, 23-4).

There is no doubt that lecturing will continue as a prime mode of teaching. The intention of this discussion is not so much to improve lecturing, although the works cited will undoubtedly be of use to those who wish to improve their skills, as to draw attention to the authoritarian tradition of our favourite method of schooling, and the extraordinary ability of the individual student to derive from it some understanding, even to be stimulated to pursue their studies. A cynic may suggest that the negative experience is such that successful students are driven to undertake more rewarding activities (such as study of texts in libraries, or discussion of issues with their peer group) which more than compensate for the grinding effect of hundreds of hours of being lectured. In reality, as Laurillard (1979) has shown, the variety of student responses to the need to take notes and of their ability to learn is so wide and so powerful that imposition of a particular methodology for note-taking would be as unwise as it is unnecessary. Does this imply that the senior teacher (who will cry — 'there, I told you so: I survived, so will they') can continue with a clear conscience to rattle off information at high speed, week after week? Surely not. Practical hints to students to help them get the best from a learning opportunity are obviously valuable. More significant than the comfort this finding may seem to offer the lazy lecturer, is the evidence concerning the nature of the learner.

Before turning to that topic, it is appropriate to talk briefly at this point about theories of learning and in particular the short and disappointing history of educational technology. The Council for Educational Technology for the United Kingdom interprets the term forming its title as being concerned 'in the broadest sense with the design of *learning systems*, drawing upon all the available methods, resources and communications media, and integrating them with established *teaching techniques* in the most effective manner to *achieve stated ends*'. The italicised phrases exemplify the problems that have always faced educational technology. The very phrase is redolent of a mechanistic approach to the experience of education, and as such is a contradiction in terms to many teachers (and as many students). The concept of applying techniques or technology to create a system that will ensure that those entering it will achieve measured gains in learning, or stated objectives, lies at the very far end of the spectrum of teaching and learning. It is an idea derived from the psychology of learning, and those who make disparaging remarks about rats in mazes or pigeons pecking pellets, when they hear the phrase 'educational technology', can be forgiven. A clear summary of the difficulties of introducing this concept into human education on a large scale, may be found at the outset of a recent publication on the psychology of learning:

> During the 1940s and 1950s, research in animal learning was one of the most popular and highly esteemed areas in psychology. The grand theories of behaviour devised during those years, best exemplified in the work of Clark L. Hull, possessed vitality, precision and breadth. In addition, the theories developed a viable technology and language within which learning principles were discovered and evaluated. Such grand schemes, however, have recently faded from the field of animal learning, largely because they were ultimately unsuccessful in their account of the many vagaries of learning which have since proved to be exceedingly extensive and complex. (Tarpy, 1975, Preface)

The most celebrated exponent of the science of learning, and its application to various aspects of education, has been B.F. Skinner. His attempts to design teaching machines led to the development of programmed learning and thereafter computer-assisted learning, which has received a kiss of life in recent years from the effect of microtechnology on computing. A passage quoted from one of Skinner's works shows why programmed learning has often seemed to be too closely reliant on psychological experiments on lower order animals:

> Some promising advances have recently been made in the field of learning. Special techniques have been designed to arrange what are called 'contingencies of reinforcement' . . . with the result that a much more effective control of behaviour has been achieved. It has long been argued that an organism learns mainly by producing changes in its environment, but it is only recently that these changes have been carefully manipulated. (Skinner, 1954, in Entwistle and Hounsell, 1975, 27)

The idea of humans as organisms whose behaviour could be controlled and manipulated, like rats in laboratories, was distasteful to many from the start. However, high hopes were expressed of the scientific approach to learning which teaching machines (later programmed texts and CAL) would achieve. The advantages of individualised study and reinforcement for successful choice of the correct answer to questions about the text presented, seem to have been weakened by the narrowness of choice of learning strategy necessarily imposed, the inappropriateness of the technique for many types of divergent study, and doubts about the amount of learning actually retained by a student using programmed material (Tarpy, 1975, 219).

Whereas educational technology as at present described involves elements of control and direction in learning that may be useful for certain kinds of study, educational television is by no means so rigidly bound. One of the misfortunes endured by educational television practitioners is that they have traditionally been associated in the minds of some critics with educational technology, and the narrow 'conditioning' mode of study with which that is linked. In reality, careful study of CET's definition of educational technology shows that the latter phrase has already been substantially widened in its scope and therefore its appeal; and educational television is expanding its own range in the 1980s to emerge as video. Nevertheless, two true stories may serve to demonstrate both why educational technology did not sweep all before it in the past decade, and how educational television was already escaping from its metallic clutches at the same time. A recent educational development, to which more detailed reference will be made later, is Sony's *Video Responder*, a device linking a video cassette recorder to a microprocessor so that video material may be programmed. In early 1982 I attended a demonstration of the device and studied a programmed video teaching elementary statistics. Soon after the start of my use of the machine I was invited by it to demonstrate my understanding of the term 'standard deviation' by calculating the s.d. for a list of numbers and typing the calculated figure. I did so, correctly, but the machine insisted I was wrong and frustratingly rewound the cassette to repeat the passage after two further 'failures'. Eventually, by trial and error, I found the (incorrect, as several colleagues confirmed) response the machine wanted and was enabled to proceed. The interesting aspect of this was not just that programs — as any computer expert will confirm — are as effective or ineffective as their programmer ('Garbage In, Garbage Out' — the GIGO principle), but that my ability to *calculate* a standard deviation accurately was a measure of my arithmetic ability (or the precision of my calculator), not of my *understanding* or *ability to use* the statistical concept. The testing was, in fact, arguably as much of an unnecessary frustration to progress as a reinforcement (even if the program had been accurate).

The second illuminating and contrasted tale relates to the development of a video-based course for first-year History students at Leeds. For the past six summer terms 60 students have studied the uses of historical evidence, by use of individual study booths in the Library where they view each week one of a set of eight videotapes made with tutors in the School of History. When the first group was about to engage in this new experience, elaborate measures were taken to prepare them: an introductory lecture (!) was delivered and students were shown that the machines were simple and easy to use. A 'surgery' rota was established, so that students who got into difficulties with the system or found learning in this way uncongenial or problematic, could have access to a tutor for personal advice. In fact the rota was abandoned within a few weeks. Three hundred and twenty students have now contentedly utilised the video material and its support literature, adopting their own strategy to use the two-hour viewing period available to them each week as they wish. A few watch and listen straight through, as for a lecture; most stop the machine frequently, inserting their own 'delightful flashes of silence'; others use the fast forward, fast rewind or even still-frame controls in idiosyncratic ways, much as they would utilise a book or a learned article. To watch them at work is to recognise how skilled, varied and complex is human learning, and how swiftly an enthusiastic mind can adapt to the challenge of an unfamiliar yet attractive mode of study.

For this author at least the truly interesting aspect of the challenge of video to established traditions lies in its potential to stimulate and support individual study, a potential summed up by the label found on at least some video recorders, 'search'. Gwen Dunn, a primary school headteacher from Suffolk, and a former member of advisory councils for both IBA and BBC, spent a year studying the significance of television in the lives of young children. She emerged with a number of striking findings about the influence of the box in the corner on the lives and perceptions of young viewers, and reinforced in her own view of education. I am glad to borrow and support this: education is a process marked above all by the desire to know, persistence through failure to success or perhaps failure again, a process that she links in her mind with Calder's statement that the most important lesson of evolutionary biology is the uniqueness of every individual (Dunn, 1980, 47).

It is a view with plenty of support for it, in terms both of respectable pedigree and recent research evidence. When Socrates was on trial for his life for 'corrupting the young', he told the jury of fellow citizens that he had been amazed at the Delphic Oracle's judgement of him, while still young, that he was 'the wisest man of all mankind'. His own interpretation of the oracular dictum was that the wisest man in the world is one who recognises, like Socrates, 'that he is worthless by the standard of true wisdom'. For Socrates also assumed that insatiable curiosity was a natural human instinct and, as mentioned above, that education is a matter of helping people to see things for themselves, not filling them full of information. His most celebrated illustration of the principle comes from the dialogue with Meno, when he asks an illiterate slave-boy a number of questions about a diagram he draws, to show that the boy in fact already 'knows' an important mathematical principle underlying the calculation of the area of a square. Leaving aside the Platonic doctrine of 'recollection', the story demonstrates Socrates' faith in the power of the mind and his respect for the individual human, as well as the usefulness, incidentally, of vision in understanding. What *is* a 'good teacher'? We might all agree that a knowledge of the subject taught and a love for it is essential, yet we have all heard or ourselves said things like 'he/she was a good teacher, but I didn't like him/her' or 'he/she was very popular, but couldn't teach for toffee'. The ideal teacher adds to the qualities of knowledge and love of the subject an element of knowledge and love for the student, which informs his/her guidance. Socrates' questions to the slave assumed no educational background such as he would have assumed for Meno (knowledge of the student); his love for the slave is clear from the patience with which he framed his questions and received the stumbling answers. One of the great benefits of computer-aided learning, which may only emerge in full as more complex programming possibilities become practicable, has been the claim of endless patience and courtesy for the disembodied teacher with whom the student develops a loving relationship. Numerous science fiction novels and stories have explored the contradictions and ethical questions posed by imbuing a robot with a personality. Such fictional possibilities may come close to reality before the end of this century, if some predictions are met.

Meanwhile, the report of a team headed by a distinguished child psychologist, Professor Michael Rutter, on eight years of research into the progress of 1,500 children at twelve London comprehensive schools, has made some intriguing and relevant points. The most significant factors in the success of a school, measured by academic achievement and low rates of truancy and delinquency, were the atmosphere of the school (i.e. its state of decoration, apparent warmth and friendliness, etc.), the attitude of the teachers (supportive in comment and systematic in teaching, rather than the opposite) and the quality of the school's administration (consultation, co-operation with teachers and checking on the quality of their work, in the better schools) (Rutter, 1979). My own summary of those findings would be that the school which provides for its pupils a learning environment most akin to that of a well-ordered, loving family home, is the one that is most likely to be successful. What is certain is that class size of itself, streaming or non-streaming, total size of school, relative size of capitation allowance, even locality and catchment area, are less influential than the factors identified.

A major element in the success of the Open University in the past decade, in attracting, retaining and educating a high proportion of the 50,000 potential students who express interest in entry each year, has been the attention it has had to give, as a distance-learning institution offering open access to higher education, to the quality of its relationship with its students. It does not always succeed, and students are forever sharing tales about the master computer's misdemeanours. My own favourite story, as a part-time tutor for the past eight years, was of the arrival, at the end of the first year of the third-level course on mass communications, of a package containing the last part of the course units of text. 'We are sorry this is a bit late', wrote the authors. 'We know the examinations are already in progress, but we thought you'd like to see the material anyway.' Well, yes, of course. Despite the inefficiency implied by that (very unusual) example of the perils of postal tuition, the key element of the Open University, as far as most students are concerned, seems to be the style, constantly being improved, of those same printed units and the attention paid to ensuring that part-time tutors and supporting radio and television material adopt the same tone. The only assumption made about the typical Open University student by the University is that he or she is highly motivated and is able, or at least willing to learn the ability, 'to learn effectively from reading, to organise study time, to set oneself study tasks and to be self-sufficient in the learning situation' (Brew, 1978, 1).

This image is a description of that 'trained mind' which every university teacher believes he or she has and also hopes his or her students will develop. It also fits well with the image of man as an endlessly enquiring figure, not a bundle of mechanically learned behaviours. George Kelly was the man who developed the idea of man-the-scientist, who interprets and transforms his/her perception of stimuli in relation to (his/her perception of) existing interpretations of the world. The individual 'constructs' reality by noticing common characteristics in some of the things perceived; the creation of the 'personal constructs' which distinguish these events from others, and contrast with them, imposes an order on the chaos of experience. A person anticipates events by construing their replications and thus interprets future reality. 'It is the future which tantalizes man, not the past. Always he reaches out to the future through the window of the present' (Kelly, 1955, 49). This model of human behaviour allows Kelly to say that 'it is not so much what man is that counts as it is what he ventures to make of himself' (Kelly, 1964, 147). So a device like the intelligence quotient is not very helpful in increasing our understanding of what people's potential performance may be, of what they can do about themselves and about each other. 'Intelligence has been regarded as a trait; . . . we should have been investigating the *process* of 'thinking', of solving problems, of construing reality' (Bannister and Fransella, 1971, 63).

George Kelly's approach to psychology and psychiatry has been paralleled by the work of Jerome Bruner in education. If the will to learn really is the most basic of human motives (survival, in fact, one might assume lies deeper still), the low motivation constantly bewailed by teachers of 'low achievers' in school is surprising. Earlier in this chapter, I referred to just such a group of 15-year olds, 'early leavers' given me, as a temporary teacher, in the final summer term of their education in 1970. My own naive hopes that I could apply strategies used in my previous experience as a teacher in a famous London private day-school, were swiftly shattered. Even the conventional bribes offered by the Headmaster for good behaviour ('a trip to London if they do as they are told for you in the next few weeks'), barely roused a flicker of interest at that stage in their rakes' progress. The only thing that really interested them (not for very long) was my connection with television, as an educational television producer. A glimmer of an idea suggested itself. I offered them a bargain. If they would work with me rather than against me, I would somehow get hold of some television recording equipment and we would together 'make some telly'. Sure enough, sleeping quietly in a cupboard at the Teachers' in-service Training Centre, several hundred pounds' worth of closed-circuit television apparatus was found. Classwork was transformed. We created three production teams, allotted roles, began to write scripts and arrange running orders, rehearsed, argued, discovered new skills and interests. The recordings eventually made revealed unsuspected strengths of character (e.g. in directing others, or planning imaginative illustration), as well as devastating weaknesses. One group ran a number of 'job interviews' for the rest of the class. The first attempt was horrific in demonstrating the awesome weaknesses of 'early leavers' as they tried to persuade a prospective employer to take them on. I needed to say very little, as often in this exercise the children criticised each other and helped each other, first to recognise that, for example, it helps if the interviewer can hear what you are saying, and then to try to do something about it.

The achievements of that short term could hardly be lasting, but they seemed to me to underline the fact that much of our schooling process concerns deluging the flame of motivation with icy water. At times the water is foul as well. In the very last week of the group's time in education, I met a queue of them outside the staff-room, in one of my rare 'free periods'. 'What is it, Jacky?' I asked the first. 'Mr Sykes is wopping us all, for cheek, like', he replied, with a sulky grin. The image of that enormous lad, three days from departure from full-time schooling, being 'wopped' by 'Mr Sykes' (a small, rodent-like, teacher of music addicted to vigorous lunch-time potations), has never left me. Jacky could easily have shaken Mr Sykes with one hand till he rattled, but he didn't: instead, he accepted from that lonely, bitter individual three blows on the back of the hand with a ruler. The authority of Mr Sykes was upheld; the mysteries of music remained dark for Jacky and his mates; the likelihood of their ever regarding education with anything more than contempt seemed very remote.

The latter part of this book discusses ways in which video seems certain to be playing, in the next 20 years, a vastly more influential role than television has done, in communication and education. Whether Mr Sykes likes it or not, the authoritarian element in schooling at every level seems likely to be reduced further by this process. There is also the possibility that education can take advantage of the rich opportunities video will afford for ingenious new learning strategies, to fan the flame of motivation in those traditionally classified as less able, and indeed to offer the high achievers more opportunity to develop their manifold skills. Before leaving Jacky and his comrades, it is important to mention the work of the Schools Council Communication and Social Skills Project, reported recently by Carol Lorac and Michael Weiss (Lorac and Weiss, 1981). Briefly, this two-year project investigated the effects that the production of audio-visual material by pupils *themselves* would have upon their learning. The authors, relying heavily on the reports of teachers who, often with some scepticism, were persuaded to involve pupils in producing curricular material in television, film, or tape/slide form, quote a great deal of qualitative evidence in support of the view that the experience did indeed enhance pupil communication and social skills, and in many cases — especially among 'less able' pupils — their understanding of the curriculum, too. The words of the independent evaluator, Lewis Owen, deserve quotation in full:

I have observed groups of children labelled of low ability, from manual working backgrounds, speaking with confidence and ease in what can only be called, if one accepts Bernstein's jargon, an elaborated code. I have seen sixteen-year-olds who confess that their film-making classes are the only ones from which they do not regularly play truant, and I have seen the same children working responsibly and collaboratively in groups, making decisions, accepting arguments and moving from leadership to the acceptance of leadership and much more. Clearly, this kind of education can dramatically change the way youngsters see themselves, and from this can develop levels of ability otherwise untapped and unsuspected. (Lorac and Weiss, 1981, 121)

This topic will be discussed in greater depth in Chapter 6. For the present it is sufficient to underline the point that the substantial boost to motivation afforded by the Project work led, as did my own experiment in 1970, to a release of co-operative energy which in turn encouraged the emergence of unsuspected skills and – in the Project at least – new intellectual achievements. Those children labelled as of 'low intelligence' (i.e. scoring low on skills measured by conventional IQ tests) tended to show particularly marked expansion of abilities in this field. 'Precisely because recorded sound and vision generate a wide range of forms of expression, pupils were able to contribute to the group learning and communication from a diverse range of individual abilities' (Lorac and Weiss, 1981, 126). The confidence they gained from the value placed by the group on their contribution led to the generation of what teachers almost unanimously agreed to be 'a high level of intellectual ability shown by children designated of low ability . . . Several teachers suggested that this work allowed low-ability pupils new access to school subjects' (Lorac and Weiss, 1981, 127). There is at least the hope, then, that one of the effects of what is being widely called the video revolution, may be a further step towards the educational aims of those who are convinced 'that men can direct their own lives, by breaking through the pressures and restrictions of older forms of society and by discovering new institutions' (Williams, 1971, 375).

The influence of the great educational psychologist, Carl Rogers, who argued that education can and should be reformed to offer greater freedom, has been growing, and imaginative use of video can contribute to this movement. A useful summary of Rogers' arguments can be found in the recent publication by the Institute for Research and Development in Post-Compulsory Education at the University of Lancaster, *How Students Learn* (Entwistle and Hounsell, 1975). It includes valuable quotations from Rogers (1969) himself and from Michael Paffard's remarkable book *Inglorious Wordsworths* (1973). In this Paffard discusses those unpredicted transcendental experiences which many great men (for example, Julian Huxley, Arnold Toynbee, Koestler, Maslow) have described as changing their intellectual and emotional lives permanently. Paffard was impressed by the number of young adult respondents to his own questionnaire on the subject who referred to such experiences in their own lives, experiences of which they had been reminded by the questionnaire itself. Paffard argues that the transcendental experience that C.S. Lewis describes in *Surprised by Joy* 'could have implications for education which too easily elude the grasp of busy reforming educators' (Paffard, 1973, 231). The Schools Council Project suggests ways in which children can be encouraged by video production to acquire skills which develop their confidence and their achievement. Gwen Dunn (1980) has described the enormous importance television already has in the lives of young children, far greater than parents or teachers appreciate. Video now presents a challenge to tradition; it is for educators to accept or deny a responsibility to reply to that challenge.

Self-initiated, self-reliant learning, as described by Rogers, can make effective use of video at all levels of study in the coming decades. If this is the result, it will mean the swift spread of the ideals of openness in education (i.e. access for all, via any route) and of continuing education. The ideal of continuing education is to regard education as a life-long quest for all of us, not a series of intellectual obstacles to be attempted by a progressively dwindling band of competitors in the first 20 years of life. Video poses a serious challenge to tradition and offers a rich opportunity for imaginative contributions to the long revolution: the challenge is part of a tide that is strong enough to break the traditions, whether or not educators wish to reform them.

2 EDUCATIONAL BROADCASTING

The concept of 'educational broadcasting', like education itself, is in process of change in the late twentieth century. Until recently, broadcasters, educators and politicians would have had little difficulty in agreeing on what was meant by the phrase. Educational broadcasting (as distinct from 'educative broadcasting', or indeed, at the other end of the scale, 'instructional broadcasting') has always been characterised by four specific features: first, acknowledged educational *purpose* (e.g. 'to contribute to the systematic growth of knowledge'); secondly, formation of the programmes into a continuous, progressive *series*; thirdly, *support* of the transmissions by other documents, whether for teachers, or students, or both; finally, investigations into the influence of the programmes by the broadcaster, so as to form the subject of *reports* to those in authority. Educational broadcasting, like education itself, has traditionally been the concern of authority and it is worth mentioning that many broadcasters, as well as a high proportion of the audience too, would add certain other points about it that are rarely made in public. Traditionally, audiences for educational programmes are relatively small, which implies that their budgets are inferior to those for entertainment and that a career in this area is rarely the prime objective of an aspiring producer or director. As a result, educational broadcasting is traditionally duller than programmes transmitted for larger audiences at peak viewing or listening periods.

The latter part of the twentieth century is seeing the transformation of these traditions, for reasons that will become clear. As part of the 'video revolution', and for other reasons, the idea that educational broadcasting must always openly acknowledge its educational purpose is in question; and certainly the principle of 'continuous series' is in doubt, as an essential prerequisite for transmissions to be classified as 'educational'. More emphasis is being given to the idea that the viewer's *reaction* or response to a broadcast is the defining factor: if viewers respond in an educational way, then the programme is educational in its outcome. Change is always painful, and these changes imply uncertainty that some broadcasters and teachers find hard to digest. If the changes lead to greater concern over the action taken after transmission, to larger audiences for programmes called 'educational' and to more resources being spent on educational broadcasting and support for it, the long-term effects will be socially very valuable. The major reason for believing that these processes will continue, and indeed accelerate, is that technical and economic forces will encourage, indeed force, them to occur. The subject is discussed in more detail in Chapter 5 below. At this point it will be sufficient to talk briefly about the dominant British and American traditions of educational broadcasting, how they have begun to change, and why. To do so it will be illuminating to look at what has been called 'the transfer of broadcasting' (Katz and Wedell, 1978, 65), that is, the way in which systems of control and production have been carried from one culture to another. Thereafter we can examine some of the obstacles to effective educational broadcasting and how attempts have been made to overcome them in the 1970s and 1980s. In Britain, as will be seen, two institutional changes in this area had a significant influence: the success of the Open University, and the arrival in 1982 of Channel Four. In other parts of the world, too, this has been a time of change for educational broadcasting.

In Britain, and in many other parts of the world, the approach to educational broadcasting had been set by the BBC. As early as 1925 the BBC appointed Miss Mary Somerville to take special responsibility for broadcasts to schools. From the first, two features marked BBC transmissions in this area: they were aimed to share excellence normally available to the more privileged sections of society with wider audiences; they were intended to offer teachers an additional resource with which to teach, rather than to teach directly. These two worthy objectives have continued to mark the great bulk of educational broadcasting in Britain, and in many other parts of the world.

The public-service model of broadcasting of which the BBC is the most famous and widely admired example is, of course, not the only possible one. The BBC's relative independence from the state is secured by its Charter, its funding from licence fees (admittedly at a level fixed from time to time by Parliament), but above all by its government through a small board of citizens who work part-time to approve, alter and sometimes initiate policy. In the field of education, the Schools Broadcasting Council, and other advisory committees drawn from a wide range of educational interests, influence the policy of the BBC's education departments. While the BBC itself produces programmes, the Independent Broadcasting Authority, which is responsible to government for the output of independent television and radio in the United Kingdom, does not. The Authority's need to assert occasional control over the commercial companies actually creating the material transmitted by the IBA, causes frequent friction between the parties concerned.

In the circumstances, it is perhaps remarkable that this friction has not been greater, and indeed, for example, that any co-operation between the IBA and BBC on educational broadcasting issues has been achieved at all.

In North America, the commercial exploitation of broadcasting has from the first been free of all but the most tenuous and occasional of central controls. Curiously, the famous phrase that is always associated with the BBC was actually first used by David Sarnoff, of RCA, who wrote in 1922 that broadcasting 'represents a job of entertaining, informing and educating the nation, and should therefore be distinctly regarded as a public service' (quoted in Briggs, 1961, 63). The British version significantly shifts 'entertain' to third position, and in reality Sarnoff's wish to develop a public-service ethos for radio was swiftly overwhelmed by the attractions of commercial sponsorship by which American traditions of broadcasting have ever since been marked. By and large, educational broadcasts had either to be so generally attractive as to compete successfully against other general output material; or they appeared on ghetto channels of their own, watched by few.

At the other end of the spectrum of traditional broadcasting models lies that centralised control which is associated with totalitarian systems of government. Both Hitler and Stalin laid great emphasis on the significance of 'education' in their broadcasting policies, and in the Third World, for quite different reasons, many states have resolved that education is too important, and broadcasting too valuable an influence, for them to relinquish the opportunity afforded by direct control of both. A three-year study of the promise and performance of broadcasting in the Third World led to the publication in 1979 of a fascinating work that offers a number of valuable insights into educational broadcasting generally. One of the most notable recurring themes of this study of the media in 91 developing countries was the growing awareness that the transfer of broadcasting models from one culture to another could carry penalties with it, alongside the benefits from proven success elsewhere (Katz and Wedell, 1978, x-xi). The authors argue that in many cases the transfer of Western models of broadcasting has not been successful in Third World countries and that imaginative change is now required to adapt or abandon these models.

The survey showed that in Africa, all broadcasting systems were modelled on European structures; in South America, most broadcasting systems were like those of the USA; in Asia, European-style systems were influenced by American approaches. The authors noted the irony that in many countries millions of dollars had been invested in expensive production and transmission equipment, without any comparable concern to ensure reception facilities. They might have added, in the context of educational broadcasting, that in the Third World the ability of students to make use of broadcast material may also be hampered by the weakness of the teaching infrastructure on which so much depends in the Western tradition. 'The trouble in Thailand', said the delegate from that country, at the World Conference on School Broadcasting in Tokyo in 1964, 'is that the teachers will turn on the sets and go fishing' (quoted in Scupham, 1967, 179). In my own experience in another developing country, although 'gone fishing' was not a problem, schools broadcasting was considerably weakened by the fact that teachers in post were often totally inadequate for the tasks set them. The 'Head of Science' in a major technical college turned out to be a young lady whose only qualification was a single A-level, in Italian! Even in Britain, despite many years of experience involving the creation of high-quality television and radio transmissions, as well as ingenious and careful support materials, there is much that is unsatisfactory about educational broadcasting. It is hardly surprising that the transfer of the system to other cultures has had mixed success.

The evidence that educational broadcasting does not work as well as might be hoped, is widespread. Despite 50 years of co-operation between broadcasters and teachers in Britain, despite the acknowledged excellence (in production terms) of British material, which regularly wins international prizes, a recent survey, one of the annual series carried out by the Scottish Education Department and the BBC, showed that the usage made by schools of educational broadcasts in Scotland was 'very patchy'. Some schools made heavy use of these expensive resources, others very little. 'Only the most popular educational series reach over 50% of their potential audiences, and the level of uptake of some series is very low indeed' (Murray, 1981, 23). When one recalls that such series are nowadays carefully planned, after taking note of teacher response to earlier transmissions, and that for some of them the 'potential audience' is therefore a selected minority one, briefed in advance, and most of them well able to record for later playback if the transmission is inconveniently timed, low uptake of this sort is very disappointing. Broadcasters may be forgiven, one might think, for developing a certain cynicism about teacher willingness and ability to use elaborate and carefully prepared audio-visual material effectively. In fact, of course, such demoralisation is very rare. Most production teams put as much creative effort and ingenuity into 'their' programmes as their budget and time allocation permits. However, the pressure of work and the attitudes of all their broadcasting colleagues inevitably influence producers towards greater interest in the *programme* than towards its *usage*. That is understandable, but it runs counter to pressures to pay more attention to the last two of the four 'specific features' of educational broadcasting mentioned at the beginning of this chapter, namely support of the programme by other materials, and reports on its influence. Just as the teacher who fails to make full use of educational broadcasts has dozens of excellent reasons why not, so the producer has a myriad of preoccupations (for example, with his or her next series!) before transmission of the new one, let alone reporting on it, is complete. It is surprising that producers do not more frequently adopt the view of the famous German scientist on this sort of issue. When questioned about his responsibility for the destruction caused by the V-bomb programme, or indeed his subsequent development of rocketry associated with ballistic missiles, he is reputed to have said that he was only responsible for designing and firing his rockets; where they fell and what their payload did, was not on his conscience! If such attitudes are ever found among educational producers, they will be reinforced by evidence that when material is produced and transmitted in short modules, on teacher advice, for more effective integration into classwork, it may then be recorded for later showing in one continuous passage to pupils. Even in 1982, educational broadcasting in Britain is bedevilled by indifference and misunderstanding on both sides of the transmitter, for all the justified admiration felt and expressed for the quality of the material often produced and its support materials.

It is important that reference to the lack of rapport between broadcaster and educator should not seem to imply criticisms of either party as having failed in some way. Nor is it suggested that this friction has not been noted and discussed in earlier contexts. For the general public, however, the reasons for the friction may be difficult to interpret. Indeed, it is difficult at times to get the parties to acknowledge that there are any problems between them at all. They are not new. As long ago as 1966, when a national conference on educational television and radio in Britain tried to examine the topic of national-local co-operation, their debate could only be reported in summary as follows:

Discussion at these sessions ranged widely, warmly and occasionally heatedly, over the range of responsibilities of the national providers and the need of the local educational system to examine thoroughly what it could get from the system and what it cannot expect to get.

It was necessary that the conference should come to grips at some stage with the nettle of mutual suspicion of the broadcaster and the educator. Many members of the conference felt this was a dying nettle and represented a false dichotomy; but all felt that many more opportunities were needed for working relationships at a practical level, involving co-operation in use and assessment. (BBC, 1966, 86)

There is no doubt that the opportunities have occurred. Doubtless, too, the mutual suspicions have decreased in the past 16 years. It is also true that there have always been considerable problems about the relationships between teacher and producer; problems that were not going to disappear through time, since they were inherent in the original concepts of 'acknowledged educational purpose' and a 'continuous, progressive series of programmes'. Both these characteristics implied an intrusion into the teacher's supreme control of classroom activities which could only be achieved in unusual circumstances.

The masterly report by C.G. Hayter (1974) entitled *Using Broadcasts in Schools* shows how affairs have begun to change. Before even beginning to discuss in detail the two million words of teacher comment (from 106 schools across the UK), the author made a most important comment about the general nature of work in the schools, a comment highly relevant to the practice of educational broadcasting: he noted that during recent years 'educational practice in many schools has moved from an emphasis on the teacher teaching to the pupils learning' (Hayter, 1974, 11). This process, which has continued to increase, at least in certain areas of curriculum, especially in the junior sectors of the state system, has been further encouraged in the past decade by the availability of more reliable and cheaper means of recording video material so that it may form an additional resource for study purposes. Once broadcast material can be recorded, stored and retrieved to enhance the understanding or learning process, it becomes enormously more valuable educationally, than if viewed on a set occasion and never seen again. Indeed, one teacher went so far as to say in 1973: 'Only when teachers are fully conversant with the contents of a series can they consider incorporating it into a scheme of work and exploiting it fully' (Hayter, 1974, 16). Hayter's conclusions from the impressive range of evidence considered, were fourfold. First, broadcasts could be very effective 'when the skill of the teacher is purposefully committed to their use, and this is most likely to happen when conditions are right'. Secondly, pre-service and in-service training could and should be strengthened to cover effective use of broadcast material. Thirdly, the recording of radio and television material was 'widely claimed' to be so valuable that the capital outlay involved in purchase of recorders was well justified; but, fourthly, the full educational utilisation of broadcast material was 'seriously restricted' by the laws on copyright.

This little matter of copyright was one of those discussed 'occasionally heatedly' at the Sussex Conference in 1966. Briefly, schools and other educational institutions in Britain are permitted to record 'off-air' BBC and ITV 'educational programmes' (not, note, 'educative programmes'), provided that the recording is made by a teacher or student in the course of instruction, is used for instruction only and only on the premises where recorded, is not copied, and is destroyed within twelve months of being made. General output programmes may only be recorded with the agreement of (a) the broadcaster, (b) the holders of any musical or literary rights, (c) the performers and (d) any gramophone companies, whose records are used in the programme. As has been pointed out many times by broadcasters, persistently besieged by educators requesting permission to use general output material, the real problems lie in contracts made between broadcasters and performers, and in the costs of satisfying the latters' demands, not in the intransigence of broadcasters themselves.

There is widespread agreement that the legal position, although the most that broadcasters can currently offer, seriously interferes with the potential educational utilisation of broadcast material. Many countries have no such copyright law as the British (1956) Copyright Act, which was drafted before video recording was ever considered a possibility for educational institutions or individual citizens. In 1977, a British government committee recommended reforms to the government. A Green Paper (consultative document) was published by the government in July 1981, a mere four years later. When one considers the pace of technological change in those four years, the response of government has been extraordinarily slow, and the document's virtual abandonment of attempts to reform the law in this area is startling.

The Educational Television Association commented on the Green Paper with regret that no real attempt had been made to come to grips with the problem of copyright. Not surprisingly, since the Association brings together all those using video for education and training, its recommendations were for recognition of the statutory right of educators to use all forms of video material for educational purposes, provided that proper reward could be offered to its creators. The

Association also underlined the importance of new technical means of recording video material (i.e. in digitalised form) and pointed out that other ingenious new developments which are relevant could confidently be predicted. It argued that a system licensing educational institutions and authorities to utilise all forms of broadcast material was required; without it, either the law would be widely flouted, or there would be a reduction in educational opportunities at the very time when technical and commercial changes were making such opportunities greater than ever before (Roach, 1982a, 87-8).

Mention has been made, both in the last chapter and again in this one in a quotation from the Hayter Report, of changes in educational attitudes and needs which are having their own effect on the concept of educational broadcasting. A perceptive and persuasive work on how broadcasting in general could and should be made more accessible to the public was Brian Groombridge's *Television and the People*, published as long ago as 1972, which is indeed a long time ago in the history of video. In it he argued that broadcasters had everything to gain, both for themselves and for the community they serve, by developing what he called 'participatory programming' approaches. It is interesting that the three examples he chose of what he meant by the phrase were all from educational broadcasting. 'Living and Growing' (Grampian Television) was a widely applauded attempt to introduce sex education to children on the edge of puberty. Before the series was made, Grampian organised an extensive range of meetings with educational administrators, teachers, clergymen and parents: a second round of meetings included the showing and evaluation of pilot programmes. This exceptional level of consultation was, of course, justified for the television company by the sensitive nature of the topic. It is interesting to note that the series has continued ever since, winning further praise for the company responsible. Harlech Television's 'Heading for a Change' was Groombridge's second example. This was an adult education series on the application of management techniques to secondary-school administration. Eight programmes went out in the region in early summer 1969, with specially convened groups meeting in secondary schools and an ingenious workbook providing viewers with a simulated 'in-tray' of typical managerial problems facing a secondary school head. The third example was the BBC's 'Representing the Union', which was designed to educate shop stewards on the subject of productivity bargaining, and depended entirely for success on the closest collaboration throughout with the Trades Union Congress (Groombridge, 1972, 179-85).

Perhaps the most significant of these three examples, since it led to a much more extensive project, was the last. Following the 1969 success of 'Representing the Union', the BBC, TUC and the Workers' Educational Association made a formal agreement which committed the BBC to produce three successive television series, over a three-year period. The collaborative nature of 'Trade Union Studies' was safeguarded by the setting up by all three organisations of a 'course team' to plan not only the broadcast element and BBC booklets, but postal courses, day-schools, weekend and summer schools for students (Matthews, 1978, 6-7). Although the complications of planning caused by this structured collaboration were considerable, it is difficult to see how the project could have achieved the credibility and influence it did without such an open acknowledgement of shared responsibility by all three agencies. The project was also noteworthy for the commitment to research and evaluation: the first series was piloted; and a research assistant studied the effect of the scheme over a period of several years. As might be expected, the results seem to have been very mixed, with some surprising failures in terms of objectives that seem to have been only rarely met, and equally startling successes (particularly in revealing to some trades union officials factors relevant to their work which they had ignored previously). Perhaps the two most important results were the surprising level of commitment and effort displayed by many students, often studying under conditions of considerable difficulty, and secondly the possibility of applying similar patterns of partnership to new adult education schemes in future. Both results derived substantially from the concept of the 'course team', to which we shall return in a moment.

During the 1970s, broadcasters in Britain have taken other initiatives to develop participatory programming policies. The BBC approach is well summarised in the annual programme for 1982-3, published by the Continuing Education department:

> Some strikingly successful collaborative projects in the last few years have involved BBC Continuing Education initiatives and a range of supporting services provided by many national and local organisations . . . The strength of such collaboration, where broadcasting acts as a catalyst or motivator for community activity, has been amply demonstrated. (BBC, 1982, 1)

Independent Television in Britain has also been trying to adapt to new social needs for educational broadcasting. A condition of acceptance of the new (1982) contracts for the programme companies was the appointment of a 'Community and Continuing Education Officer'. The hope is that, once this condition has been fulfilled, the commercial network in Britain may be able to take advantage of its federal nature to support national campaigns with locally appropriate activities, planned in consultation with a range of other agencies. One experiment of the late 1970s, derived from an American idea but translated to the British context, was an educational reaction to a general output programme. With IBA assistance, a group of academics, members of the press and local radio and regional educators and educational experts, worked with the local commercial television company, Yorkshire Television, to create a pilot 'pack' of educational material as follow-up to a popular historical drama. ATV had produced a four-part romantic drama based on the life and loves of Benjamin Disraeli; when screened in Yorkshire and Humberside, viewers were invited at the end of transmission to 'write off to this address if you'd like to receive some information about some of the topics covered in this play'. The pamphlet sent to those who asked for it included material on Disraeli himself (especially about his visits to Yorkshire) and a number of places to visit where (by pre-arrangement) the programme's 'Dizzy' symbol attracted the reader to displays, activities or other educational opportunities. The experiment was mounted on a limited budget and the authors of the pamphlet recognise its weaknesses, but the response (from a wide spectrum of society) was high enough to cause the Director of the National Extension College, the most celebrated correspondence course institution in Britain, himself a member of the group, to refer to this experiment with enthusiasm long after its conclusion.

Earlier, I referred to the Open University and to Channel Four as having had considerable influence on trends in educational broadcasting in the latter portion of this century. Many educational broadcasters would disagree, but in retrospect both institutions will be seen as significant forces, in quite different ways. The importance of the OU in this context has been that it has demonstrated that the 'course team' approach to the production of educational material (both print and television, as well as radio or audio-cassette and experimental work, if appropriate) is feasible: broadcasters have been quite as sceptical as teachers about this possibility. The University also from the first laid heavy emphasis on the importance of evaluation and research with part of its Institute of Educational Technology working permanently on the assessment of particular courses' success, so as to recommend future improvements. These recommendations have not always been heeded; sometimes pressures have prevented their even being properly read by those in power; but the concept of research (that fourth factor defining a broadcast as 'educational') as an expected, essential concomitant to the broadcast, rather than an occasional ritual addition to a particularly complex or novel series, has been one of the features of the University's work which has most impressed overseas visitors.

Senior staff from the Open University formed Channel Four's educational management when the first new broadcasting channel in Britain for 25 years began its preparations for launch in 1982. It is widely expected that they will wish to bring to that new channel some of their experiences from the Open University. In any case, Channel Four has an unparalleled commitment to education (15 per cent of total output) written into its required transmission arrangements and the unique role (for Britain) of commissioning its material from anyone who can satisfy production and technical standards, and has a good enough idea to offer. That is the claim and that is the intention of the Channel's management. How novel the Channel's output will eventually turn out to be, and how well watched, remains to be seen. The interest of the venture for educational broadcasting lies in the prominence given to educational purposes in the Channel's schedules and the emphasis already being given to what is called 'follow-up', that is, the production and dissemination of information or publications about activities to follow the viewing experience. On this topic, the constraints of finance have been stressed by the Managing Director, who has publicly referred to this aspect of Channel Four's activities as a 'publishing programme' which would be 'self-financing, if not profitable' (Media Project, 1982a, 5). Publications derived from transmissions, of course, may indeed be profitable, even educational publications. It is well known that 'Botanic Man', an educational series produced by Thames Television in 1980, was one of the most successful ventures in the history of British educational broadcasting, with very large audiences indeed: this was due not only to the excellence of the production but to the investment of a substantial production budget for the series, as well as the earmarking of a regular peaktime slot for transmission. The sales of support materials (as well as international sales of the series) have no doubt amply justified the investment. Sales of the BBC/Collins publication *Life on Earth*, based on enormously successful television series, exceeded one million and it is estimated that the presenter/writer alone received £1 in royalties for each copy sold. With potential spin-off profits of this size, it is no wonder that the Managing Director of

Channel Four can regard 'follow-up' as a profitable business, for all its innovative intent. Nor should educators necessarily blanch at the prospect of educational broadcasting being regarded as part of a business, instead of an inevitable drain on broadcasting revenues. If the shift in attitude leads to better transmission slots and larger budgets for educational programmes, the changes will be widely welcomed. In the United States, even material for ethnic minorities is now actively marketed to commercial broadcasting stations with growing success (Lloyd-Kolkin, 1981).

Something should be said at this point about social action broadcasting. This topic has consistently been bracketed with educational broadcasting, much to the irritation of those involved in social action broadcasting, and mainly for the weak reason that no other convenient administrative category has yet been found for it, despite attempts to accord it an administrative classification of its own in broadcasting. Broadly speaking, 'social action broadcasting' involves co-operation between broadcasters and voluntary or statutory agencies responsible for some aspect of social welfare. In Britain in May 1982, several hundred such programmes or slots within programmes were listed by the Media Project in their Directory. All involved or affected the work of one or more agency and most had an element of follow-up: a listener or viewer is stimulated by the transmission to contact the agency concerned to get advice, information or to offer assistance. In addition to special programmes or slots, broadcasters may refer to social welfare topics in general output programmes (e.g. dramas or documentaries) with the expectation that the agency concerned will be able to cope with the subsequent reaction from the public. Since Channel Four has expressed a strong commitment to programming on a number of social welfare issues, it might be expected that the channel would have made special provision to cover some of the problems that can be predicted (and to offer some prospect of taking advantage of many new opportunities) for the voluntary and statutory agencies. However, as of early 1982 'the chances of their being a back-up unit staffed by numbers of efficient people who do nothing else but look out for this kind of thing at Channel Four is extremely remote, not to say non-existent' (Liz Forgan, Senior Commissioning Editor, Current Affairs and Factual Programmes, Channel Four, quoted in Media Project, 1982a, 5). There is an undeniable difficulty here: broadcasters understandably see their role as spending resources on broadcasting, not on activities following broadcasting; agencies having to cope with demands for which they have no additional resources tend to resent this attitude. The friction and misunderstandings noted earlier between broadcasters and educators are found here again; to that extent, social action broadcasting can be categorised as similar to educational broadcasting, particularly in its most recent manifestations.

In both cases, these problems can only be resolved by the release of new energies and resources, either from public funds (unlikely, but, given the social and economic forecasts for the nature of the post-industrial society, not unthinkable) or through finding ways of co-operation hinted at by the development of the course team concept, in areas other than the academic. Perhaps the most significant influence towards change in this area is change itself. Broadcasting is facing unprecedented challenges to its methods of managing itself and its audiences. It is quite possible that within a decade traditional BBC dominance of, say, sports reportage or news, will have disappeared; it is perfectly possible that the traditional ITV financial resource, commercial advertising, will have dwindled to a fraction of its current level. The latter was at an all-time high in 1982, but that seems unlikely to last, under the impact of cable, satellite, videocassette and videodisc. Net revenues from independent television advertising in Britain rose by 15 per cent in 1981 over 1980, and rose by up to twice that percentage increase in 1982 over 1981. The two broadcasting services cannot expect total control of public viewing, already slipping away, to remain for much longer, and as it decreases advertising revenue is bound to fall as well; licence revenue, the BBC's meat and drink, is hardly likely to expand in real terms in such a situation. In what Brian Wenham, the controller of BBC-2, called 'The Third Age of Broadcasting', the British broadcasters will have to adapt swiftly and imaginatively if they are to survive (Wenham 1982). Those that do survive to continue to produce educational material will do so by devising new forms of television which only have full impact when viewed in the context of other published material, probably depending for its utilisation on agreements even more complex and far-reaching than that between BBC, TUC and WEA for 'Trade Union Studies'. Educational broadcasting in Britain is therefore bound to change; it may indeed almost disappear; but the function it has fulfilled will remain and shrewd planning may mean that educational broadcasters, widely and rightly admired for their achievements, can play a vital role in the Third Age that is almost upon us.

3 EDUCATIONAL TELEVISION UNITS

The future of educational broadcasting seems likely to have much in common with the more successful aspects of the work of educational television units in future years. What are 'educational television units'? How successful have they been, in their much briefer history, extending as it does over a mere 15 or so years? What lessons can be learned from their successes and failures, that may be useful for the video era? What role could they play in that era?

The Educational Television Association, referred to briefly in the previous chapter, brings together institutions and individuals using television for education and training. An educational television unit is therefore any service or unit staffed and equipped to create television material (or to distribute or adapt it) to support trainers or teachers in their work. Most British universities have some form of central service unit with this kind of responsibility, as do almost every university, institute and college in North America. In Britain other typical units are found in polytechnics, colleges, some hospitals, and in training branches of industrial, police and armed service organisations. Each of these units is unique in staffing, responsibilities and equipment, as befits educational systems as individualistic as Western ones. The influence of a particular personality or of a particular institutional tradition has had remarkable effects in some cases, skewing the role of the unit at one institution towards concentration on activities almost totally ignored at equivalent institutions in other parts of the country. This has been particularly noticeable in educational institutions, where the concept of 'academic freedom' or 'teacher freedom' has led to anomalies and eccentricities the more startling when one considers the pre-history of educational television units. As will emerge, the individualism that has so influenced the work of these units in the past 15 years is in sharp contrast to the national planning that was so much in the air when they were created. At that time educational television units in Britain were seen as playing a role similar to that of educational broadcasting in the Third World, and there are interesting parallels between the history of both over the intervening period.

If in what follows there seems to be particular concentration on the history of educational television units in universities, this will not only be because that is where my own experience lies but because that is where the most striking and illuminating examples for this topic may be found. Much of what is said applies *a fortiori* to other educational television units elsewhere, however different their purpose and circumstances. It is difficult, in the context of 1982, fully to appreciate the heady expectations for educational television that were being trumpeted in 1966, only 16 years ago. The National Conference on educational television and radio in Britain held in that year at the University of Sussex made predictions and moved in a tide of confidence that has ebbed rapidly almost ever since. The word 'national' in the title of the Conference is significant: references throughout repeat the adjective. The 'National Plan' required education to provide for Britain's economic needs; the Robbins Report on the expansion of higher education was seen as part of that provision. Speakers referred to the aim of particular university television units as to 'cover approximately 10% of undergraduate teaching' within five years, and to the implications of the arrival of such units as being 'a new approach to the deployment of teaching resources, and a rationalisation of manpower', leading to the prospect of 'offering recorded material to other universities'. Above all, there was heavy emphasis on the need for educators 'to rethink the traditional techniques and purposes of teaching' so as to maximise the new medium. The conference seemed to digest all this without too much difficulty, and proceeded to recommend at several points the establishment of a National Centre to co-ordinate the production, cataloguing and exchange of material, as well as appropriate training of educators and audio-visual staff. Little of this in fact developed, and even where institutional provision was made (there was indeed, for example, soon a National Council for Educational Technology, as well as a National Council for Audio-Visual Aids in Education, a National Educational Closed-Circuit Television Association and a British Universities Film Council), the co-ordinating power of these bodies was minimal. Within the universities themselves, the predicted impact of the educational television units was not as great as had been expected.

Why was this? The first Director of the largest educational television service in a British university saw three major problems facing the new closed-circuit television systems in 1966: first, equipping and operating the unit at a satisfactory technical standard; secondly, 'encouraging teaching staff to understand the quite new dimension of communication that television makes possible and that its proper use makes inevitable a new approach to the teaching process'; thirdly, co-ordinating and rationalising the new units, in order to avoid duplication and 'haphazard growth'. Few would have disagreed in 1966; indeed, few would do so now. Sadly, all three problems have remained serious obstacles to the 'proper use' of television for education and training. There is one underlying reason for comparative failure in all three areas, and that is embodied in the second of the three problems noted. Academic staff welcomed the Robbins expansion and the arrival of educational television to assist in coping with it, with varying degrees of enthusiasm. Some of the most powerful figures in higher education tended towards the sceptical, even hostile end of the spectrum. The arrival of figures from the world of broadcasting without the same academic ethos as their own, requiring them to 'understand' that a new dimension of communication was upon them, implying an inevitable 'new approach to the teaching process' did not go down well. Even where academics were not so bluntly told that they could and should change their long-established ways, the new units faced crucial problems in this area, which had and still have considerable influence on their work. In the other two areas identified, relationships with the teachers who control universities were also responsible for the difficulties undergone in the following decade. Some units managed to achieve first-class technical standards (perhaps by dint of securing a friendly link with a local broadcasting station); others achieved staffing levels which permitted effective operational crewing; few, if any, maintained both. The underlying reason for this was the failure of the institution to make use of the unit effectively, a failure of relationships which was self-sustaining. The third major problem identified, national co-ordination, remains unsolved. The 1966 Brynmor Jones Report on Audio-Visual Aids in Higher Scientific Education recommended that 15 of the 45 British universities should set up central services, each creating television material for others in the neighbourhood. Despite strenuous efforts by the central units themselves, university departments by and large expressed little interest in other institutions' materials and, indeed, by 1971 a total of 35 (later 43) universities had in fact set up their own television units. This almost certainly had more to do with academic freedom to do one's own thing than with evidence of success within the original high-activity centres.

Academic freedom is a noble concept. Like certain other fine ideals, it is quoted rather too frequently to excuse unreasonable behaviour or to justify pigheadedness. Where the ideal protects the liberty of the teacher or researcher to quote or seek truth, no democrat would deny its power; where it allows powerful departments to evade investigation or reform, or even enquiry, it becomes licence rather than liberty. Educational television units' recommendations may have occasionally been tactlessly expressed, and their predictions may have seemed overconfident, but they accorded well with national and social needs as generally seen at the time, and could have been expected to attract active support from within the universities served. In fact, the educational television units tended to become relatively isolated as many university departments found they could cope with the Robbins expansion without the irritating need to change their familiar methods of teaching, since abundant public funding permitted recruitment of academic staff to maintain traditional staff/student ratios and methods. There were exceptions. In medical and engineering training, in particular, there were remarkable examples of co-operation between imaginative teachers and ingenious producers, who overcame technical and other obstacles to create material of lasting value. Generally the central problem was untouched. No conventional British university, at least to my knowledge in the first decade from 1966, set up anything resembling an ongoing course team of academics and educational television staff as at the Open University, to devise television and textual material for a particular curricular area. Certainly, there were no large-scale regional or national exercises to create materials in this sort of way and no unit achieved a contribution of anything like coverage of 10 per cent of all undergraduate teaching.

These comments will be read by some as unfair criticism of academics, by others as unreasonable criticism of the actual achievements of the units themselves. It is easy to seem wise after the event. Even armed with hindsight it is doubtful if one's own track record would have been markedly better. It is, however, worth noting and emphasising that the central problem lay and lies in the educational model which informs practice in Britain and most other countries. While the teacher is seen as a figure of secret authority, expert in arcane bodies of knowledge which can only gradually be revealed to apprentices, the intervention of a third party whose role is to familiarise himself or herself with those mysteries and then to assist in presenting them to an enormously widened audience, is bound to seem to threaten the magus. In the early years of educational television units, a further obstacle to development was the technical complexity of production. Even if a teacher rashly agreed to create new material, the experience of working for hours under hot lights and away from one's own department was discouraging and often decisive in putting off the new recruit. The fact that many of the new members of staff in the units had come from broadcasting backgrounds did not improve matters: their impatience with academic precision and foibles added to the friction between the parties. The association of educational television units with a host of activities and events regarded as undesirable by conservative academics did not help matters. Senior academics had reaped and continued to award promo· tion and prestige primarily for research achievement; the central units were almost exclusively concerned with teaching. Universities in Britain had traditionally been responsible to their own governing body and resented the imposition of regional or national objectives; the stance of the units tended to be one of communicating and interpreting academic messages to the outside world in part fulfilment of social objectives set by the community. Many academics regarded broadcast television in the 1960s as frivolous, even dangerous, in its effect on the lives of their families and their students; here was a unit, a 'tee-vee' unit, actually on campus, staffed by ex-broadcasters; horror of horrors!

These problems recurred elsewhere in the educational system, except where television units were set up to carry out highly specific tasks, generally some aspect of training, for a specialised public service or commercial purpose. Despite the unexpected difficulties faced by the new units, some impressive achievements were made, not only in the production of audio-visual media of every kind, but in organising and distributing software, providing training and advice, and, in ways sometimes unrecognised at the time by unit and co-operating teacher, above all in developing novel teaching and study strategies. During the past 15 years those responsible for the work of these units have become influential figures in the world of educational technology, achieving, publishing and learning more and more about the ways and means of applying new techniques to improve education. In the past five years or so the beginnings of the technological revolution have considerably assisted their work, by offering cheaper, more reliable and easier access for teachers and students to video material. Production and editing equipment has also become less expensive and less bulky, more reliable and more flexible, raising standards and offering teachers greater and more easily won rewards for their investment of time and effort. New libraries in higher and further education in the past few years have been equipped with videocassette recorders to enable students to utilise television material on a par with the way they have traditionally used books and learned articles. In some rare cases entire courses have been prepared and offered with television as a major compulsory component. Such initiatives are not at all common in Britain, although they are well-known in North America. Medical training at pre-clinical level has made particularly heavy use of television resources, to the extent that some universities recruited fewer additional members of staff in recent

expansions, relying on television as a communication device to offer
students in very large classes of up to 200 a detailed view of a lecturer
or demonstrator at work, and a limited opportunity for feedback. A
rich, in some cases irreplaceable, storehouse of materials was created
and developed during this period, increasingly for use in the library or
department by small groups of students or individuals, rather than as
illustrations inserted into lectures.

Reference was made earlier to the comparison possible between
the history of educational television units and educational broadcasting in developing countries. The authors of *Broadcasting in the Third
World* make the link themselves, when they talk of the enthusiasm for
educational technology in the developed world infecting the Third
World even more powerfully in the 1960s. Their own interpretation of
the cause of this enthusiasm was that it derived

> on the one hand from the wish to modernise traditional educational
> methods and on the other from the hope that less labour-intensive
> teaching methods might help to reduce the unit cost of education
> at a time of massive expansion of educational opportunities through-
> out Europe and North America. (Katz and Wedell, 1978, 120)

Just as such expectations in the developed world were foiled by resistance to change and inherent technical and psychological obstacles,
the promise of educational television for the Third World appears not
to have been matched by its performance. Does this prove that the
initial plans were misguided, in either case? Not necessarily. Expensive
and relatively disappointing though these developments have been, they
were not nearly so costly as some other projects from 20 years ago, and
what has been learned from them can now be applied confidently at a
time when technical advances and educational needs are shifting in
favour of the application of television to the solution of many more
educational problems. The topic of Third World adaptation will come
up again in the final chapter of this book.

One of the major difficulties facing educational television units in
institutions over the years has been the disturbance of the traditional
relationship between teacher and student that is implied by the production of these materials. More disturbing still has been the implicit
encouragement of the idea that students themselves can react to and
assess teaching material, even perhaps suggesting modifications. Such a
prospect, well known in medical training, and widespread in North
America, is anathema to the approach of most European and Asian or

African teachers to their role. This factor has been a very significant obstacle to the progress of educational television units, in addition to others which in any case militate against the whole process of innovation in teaching. In a perceptive article, summarising several years of work by the Open University Institute of Educational Technology, Angela Brew recently discussed some of the reasons for the relatively small range of innovations found in higher education over the 1970s. Despite clear research evidence, available for more than ten years, that lecturing is an inefficient method of changing attitudes or stimulating understanding (Bligh, 1972), the lecture remains a teaching mode of choice for teachers around the world, used to satisfy a great variety of intellectual purposes in universities, colleges and schools. For more than 20 years we have known, if we had forgotten our own experiences, from the clearest evidence, that students' ability to take notes precisely and fully is inadequate (e.g. Hartley and Cameron, 1967). Yet note-taking is assumed to be an inherent, natural skill which every student possesses. Numerous pieces of evidence from a great variety of sources have shown the variety of students' approaches to study, implying the wisdom of providing a variety of learning opportunities to any group, however able and well-motivated (e.g. Laurillard, 1979). Yet organisation of study opportunities is far rarer than instruction of large groups, in higher education. If the relatively straight-forward innovations implied by attention to such clear evidence have not led to change, is it surprising that resistance to the more radical changes demanded by some of those trying to introduce educational television to higher education has been persistent and powerful? The illuminating aspect of the cited study by Brew is that it suggests, perceptively and convincingly, that this resistance is not due to conservative obduracy so much as to the teacher's perspective of problems facing him or her, and of the relevance of this or that innovative approach to resolving them (Brew, 1982, 160). It is not, in fact, a question only of integrating a suggested innovation (whether methodology or material) into teaching, but of how the teacher conceives both the problem and the potential resolution of it offered by the proposed innovation. These complementary perspectives, the actual potential contribution and its perception, it is suggested, need to be considered together to explain why the process of change appears to be so very slow.

In any case, the purpose of this discussion has not been to apportion blame for this or that relative failure, but rather to describe events hitherto and outline potential future contributions. One very important point which has to be made is that it is only a matter of five or six years that educational television units have been able to claim with a straight face that working with them is not only straightforward, but leads to the creation of material that can be made available in a 'user-friendly' form. The phrase is borrowed from the language used by computing which until recently also tended to claim more for itself as a learning tool than was found to be the common experience. In the 1960s educational television material was seen as offering the opportunity to teach overflow classes, to demonstrate detail, to train teachers and to repeat excellent lectures to other groups (Brynmor Jones, 1965). There is no doubt that all four functions have been proved possible, but an inherent necessary weakness is their being seen – as the government report from which they are quoted put it – as *aids* to the teacher. The most fascinating and promising aspect of the experience of the last few years is the technical and conceptual shift towards creation of material for direct use by the clients, i.e. the students. The great beauty of this shift, apart from the educational values discussed in the first chapter of the book, is that it removes the psychological challenges posed by working to produce 'aids for the teacher'. Ironically, although many teachers claim that is what they require, they are unable in reality to cope with the interference to the relationship with 'their' students implied by the intervention of a third party, whether a television producer or an expert colleague from elsewhere. One of the most celebrated British academic economists was once shown a carefully made piece of television, created by a junior colleague in his own department, illustrating a point first conceived by the great man himself. 'Fascinating', he murmured, 'but I wouldn't teach it that way myself.' Perhaps not, and as long as the innovative material is offered as an aid to teaching, the teacher has the right to reject it. What if it is offered as an aid to study? Teachers are well used to this concept, from senior secondary school level upwards. 'You might have a look at Smith's attempt to explain this theory in video form. It's a valiant try.' This kind of comment is parallel to invitations to 'have a look at' this or that written text or article, which for all its faults, is still 'worth study'. Once the material is available as a resource for study it becomes user-friendly, to teacher as well as student.

We are still some way from total 'friendliness', of course. Developments in video technology that form the main theme of this book are designed above all for the consumer market. Generally when a video manufacturer claims to have designed something for the much smaller educational market, it is wise to examine the claims very carefully before committing scarce resources to purchase of equipment which past experience suggests will have rapid obsolescence. Putting this point more plainly, the educational 'market' is sometimes seen as a useful dumping area for sales of obsolete or near obsolete devices once general consumer resistance is being predicted or a new device is in production. This is a surprising attitude when the immense, but sadly divided, buying power of educational television units, and increasingly the teaching departments or libraries they advise and assist to buy, is considered. There is a very big market indeed, and one that will not be subject to the roller-coaster effects for which wider markets are notorious, open to a manufacturer wishing to design a truly 'user-friendly' video device for educational purposes.

What would such a device be like? The editor of the *Journal of Educational Television* described the perfect machine for individual study in the following terms, in an article reviewing nearly 20 years of publications on the subject of television for education and training:

Imagine a rectangular box, about 35cm wide, 25cm high and 7.5cm deep. The front of the box is largely occupied by a television screen (of the flat, solid-state type), plus a row of touch-sensitive controls. The right-hand side of the box is vertically slotted. Into this slot the student slips a video-disc, perhaps 17.5 cm in diameter, giving a 20-minute programme per side . . . The machine presents moving and still (true still) pictures as required and is completely flexible as far as direction of programme is concerned — random access in fact. All our requirements are now met, and more. By incorporating a microprocessor, and linking playback of the disc to computer-guided sequencing, including generated graphics, we have a complete learning machine, able to organise learning on a fully individualised basis. Now we're getting somewhere! (Roach, 1980, 76)

We shall return to the utilisation of such a device, or of something like it, in Chapter 7. At this point, we shall only describe in brief the sort of material that the developments of the past five years have typically seen in educational television units. These can be said to be characterised by increase of precision and reduction of marginal costs. In medicine, for example, pre-clinical training, as well as relying on television for communication of illustration, has also been strengthened by the creation of a large amount of material that can demonstrate, say, the physiological responses of an experimental animal to a large group without having to supply each student or pair of students with a specimen. The reduction of cost, and indeed of experimental activity, is considerable.

In clinical medicine, some dangerous conditions are now rarely seen, but the recognition of their signs remains a vital part of a doctor's training. Television has provided a ready resource to build up an invaluable catalogue of rare presentations; even with much more frequently observed conditions there is an obvious increase in efficiency, through reduction of lecturer, student and patient time, by recording in full colour and sound the detailed examination of a particular case. In the long term, as discussed later, the development of libraries of this kind of material affords prospects of increasing the reliability of training and indeed of the public examination of students. There will also be more concentration on such relatively neglected areas as the doctor-patient relationship, increasingly seen as a vital component in the interpretation of health and the application of effective therapy.

Medicine offers the most striking examples of the usages of television in higher education. The medical profession is one that particularly lends itself to audio-visual description, with that combination of long experience, skilled observation with eye, ear and hand, and precise intellectual judgement which marks the ideal practitioner at work. Lecturers in medicine and surgery were among the earliest and have always tended to be among the most energetic and imaginative users of television in the academic world. Yet even their utilisation could be very considerably extended, with beneficial effect. In particular, certain practices that the public understandably assumes are standardised and agreed, have been shown to exhibit a wide variety of performance which is both unnecessary and dangerous. When a videotape made several years ago by an anaesthetist to train nursing staff in emergency procedure in a busy city infirmary, was shown at the time to colleague anaesthetists in the same hospital, it provoked a storm of protest concerning this or that procedure. Even the protest was *itself* divided. Each anaesthetist claimed his approach was the only safe one and accused colleagues of errors in their practice. Television had succeeded, quite unintentionally, in spotlighting potentially dangerous divisions which would otherwise have remained undetected; one wonders in how many other fields of clinical practice this may be true. On another occasion an opportunity arose to compare one recording of a lecturer describing 'the examination of the total patient' with a recording of another lecturer in the same medical school delivering a lecture/demonstration on the identical topic in the same term. There were striking differences of approach and detail (including omissions) obvious even to a lay viewer. The full-scale examination of a patient suggests itself as a prime theme for national or even international training, since it is manifestly straightforward and routine in nature yet of considerable, occasionally vital, importance. Retraining of professionals such as doctors is an expensive and problematic activity: educational television as yet plays a minor role in it. Why so? Probably once again because of the problem of relationships referred to more than once in this chapter. The educational television unit concerned has raised this sort of subject again and again with teachers and deans of faculty responsible, without result. Standardisation of this nature seems to be regarded at present as an intrusion on academic freedom and professional independence, whatever the effect of its absence on patient care. In the long term the technical shift from television to video will overcome obstacles here, as elsewhere, no doubt.

In engineering training, especially mechanical and civil engineering, there are similarities to medical training which have encouraged considerable use of educational television in the past 15 years. One of the earliest examples, at the University of Leeds, was the recording of an entire series of videotapes designed to free a demonstrator from the tedious role of preparing group after group of first-year or second-year students to carry out standard observations and measurements on machines. Each tape introduced the particular machine itself, showed it in action, performing its regular function, and demonstrated how to calibrate and read instruments to measure its performance: the recording was shown to the group, who then took prepared test sheets away on which to enter their own observations when they ran the machine. This procedure was utilised for over a decade, until the videotapes quite literally wore out. They have saved thousands of hours of skilled technician time, while providing an absolutely reliable presentation on each occasion. More recently, individual students have been offered library access to recordings of experiments which are extremely costly and lengthy to mount, rather than require large groups to attend once-for-all demonstrations for which their viewing position may be quite inadequate. Once again, standardisation is possible, and of course students may proceed at their own pace, so that the more able will perhaps view the material once, while less able ones may view the demonstration several times, repeating particular passages as many times as necessary. Slow motion and stop-frame facilities have recently been incorporated into inexpensive video recorders, offering new opportunities for individual insight and interpretation impossible with traditional methods.

It will not have escaped the reader's notice that all the examples quoted are of material that is readily transferable within a society, and indeed exportable to other communities, with appropriate translation into other languages, if similar needs for training have to be met there. In case it should be thought that educational television is inherently antipathetic to the traditions of tutorial or seminar study that are perhaps the greatest glory of educational organisation in our culture, it should be added that some of the most intriguing usages developed by members of the Educational Television Association in the past decade have been devoted to stimulus of just such activities. Management training, of course, may itself include the study of 'in-tray' materials which are then discussed or which initiate group responses. Such simulations were mentioned earlier when reference was made to Harlech's 'Heading for Change' series as an early example of 'participatory' educational broadcasting. Similar examples abound in the records of educational television units. Sometimes training of individual professionals by use of simulation can be used at a later stage to encourage seminar work: a good example is the recording of individual students coping with a (simulated) real-life application of their skills, for later analysis not only by the student with the tutor, but by other groups of students in future years. This sort of recording can be envisaged as part of a package of learning materials for use in a great variety of situations and to satisfy different, indeed individual purposes: it is probably the most important single growth area for educational television in the next few years.

The potential role of these units in the video industry is immense. The original problems posed by technical clumsiness and by psychological barriers preventing ready teacher usage of audio-visual material are dissolving at the same time as demands for more varied forms of education and training from all sectors of society are increasing rapidly. Their potential contribution to new patterns of education is discussed in greater detail in the latter part of this book. Three factors that are relevant to the realisation of that potential or not, need to be considered, and no doubt can be parallelled in other parts of the world. First, the climate of turmoil in education spells dangers for the survival of these units, given the inherent problems of relationship which have been stressed. Some of those same administrators and teachers who opposed the formation of such units in their institutions 15 or 20 years ago, are still in power, sometimes in even more influential positions. The need to reduce costs is being used by some institution managements as an excuse for paying off old scores and closing down or phasing out units at the very moment when their unique experience and new position of promise should be of immense value. Secondly, most of the running in the microtechnology race is being made by computers and computer salesmen. There is a real possibility that the educational potential of television will not be fully realised in the age of video because of the undeniably enormous value of computing techniques and the strength of, for example, the computer-based learning lobby that has been given a new lease of life by the micro revolution. Finally, and most important of all, these units, in terms of staff composition, experience and natural links with professional allies, are a uniquely valuable resource to assist in the redevelopment of educational institutions in the late twentieth century. More than any other department or service in a polytechnic or university, the educational television unit, where it exists, has had an unparallelled range of educational responsibilities, and experience peculiarly well suited to those principles of openness, adaptability and continuing education that will be the hallmark of late twentieth-century learning. An eloquent document produced by the Council for Educational Technology in 1979 lucidly summarises the contribution of these central service units to higher education, and to wider social needs, in the 1990s (CET, 1979). A quotation from this document aptly closes this section by underlining the special role that can already be claimed for these units in British education: the crucial phrase in the second sentence refers to the need for adequate institutional commitment. One can predict that those institutions that apply imagination, energy and resources to these purposes will reap a rich advantage over their decaying rivals, in the not too distant future.

> The higher education system has already made considerable provision for the application of educational technology through the establishment of central institutional facilities . . . Costs can be reduced, providing there is adequate institutional commitment to achieving this aim; changes in course patterns can be facilitated, with educational technology playing a major role. (CET, 1979, 1-2)

The role of the Educational Television Association in stimulating, monitoring and providing a forum for discussion of progress in the area, is similarly very bright indeed, if it can survive the era of retrenchment.

Part Two

VIDEO, COMMUNICATION, EDUCATION

4 VIDEO AND COMMUNICATION

> What we are now grappling with is radical precisely because it presents a technological change in the way of building electronics which reduces the cost by a factor of at least a thousand — perhaps more — and improves its reliability so greatly that failure rates are no longer an effective limitation on system complexity. (Gosling, 1978, 14)

In case there are still any readers who are completely at sea over the term microelectronics, it will be as well to explain very briefly why the developments referred to above in Professor William Gosling's influential lecture, 'The Kingdom of Sand', are so often called revolutionary. The discovery that integrated electronic circuits can be reduced to microscopic size photographically and then locked into a fragment of solid, inert, crystal which has an indefinite life, is the transforming cause of the turmoil we are experiencing in electronics and those many parts of society the industry already affects. The process was described theoretically 30 years ago, achieved in the 1960s, and continues to accelerate with progressively more dramatic miniaturisation. The greatest increases in power and collapses in cost have so far been seen in computing; one of the reasons for looking at the implications for video is that the pace of change is so great that there is a danger of losing control of events. As Professor Gosling, now Director of Research with one of Britain's largest electronics manufacturers, has himself put it, 'the only thing that could conceivably cheat us is the poverty of our own capacity to imagine' (Gosling, 1980, 85).

Television is changing rapidly, in ways that are sometimes difficult to observe, yet enormously influential. We have already seen the arrival of teletext, the BBC's 'Ceefax' and ITV's 'Oracle' systems, affording a range of possible new information services to supplement the familiar broadcast material. This development is one example of changes that will dramatically affect our use of television receivers in the near future. Another is the availability of those receivers themselves. Miniaturisation, reduced price and increased reliability have already swept through the calculator and wristwatch markets; precisely the same developments are bound to affect the television industry in the not-too-distant future. This will be one of the factors considered in detail below. Other effects that are particularly relevant to communication concern the storage and transmission of information itself and the part video will play in that area of communication.

Professor Gosling addressed the Educational Television Association on this subject in 1979, and his views form a useful introduction to consideration of the role of video in communication in the late twentieth century. He described three major steps in the transformation of television, steps that are already being taken, and which are already affecting the industry, but which most of us can barely imagine. First, the evolution of microelectronics production has not yet run its full course. The *New Penguin Dictionary of Microelectronics* (Young, 1979, 242) refers under 'integrated circuit' not only to very large-scale integration (circuits with a complexity between 16,000 'bits', single yes-no decisions between equiprobable choices, up to 1,000,000 bits) but to extra large-scale integration (over 1,000,000 bits per chip). VLSI chips are already in production: 256K random access memory (RAM) chips have been manufactured at several laboratories since 1980 (Frons and Willenson, 1982, 30). The goal of the first megabit (1,000,000 bits) chip in production will be achieved shortly, and thereafter ELSI RAMs are conceivable. At the same time as this accelerating miniaturisation continues, the speed of operation of the circuitry involved continues to increase. Research in Japan is concentrating on the development of chips 'five times as powerful as the most advanced experimental models made, with processing ability ten times faster than the most powerful computers on the market' (Ramsey and Willenson, 1982, 34). It is difficult for the ordinary citizen to appreciate what research of this kind (aimed at creating a computer brain with the ability to infer, and to work on several types of 'thought' at once, an aim the sponsors readily acknowledge may not of itself be achieved) is likely to mean in social terms. Professor Gosling's words are visionary, yet he unerringly puts his finger on the central issue for society, to which we shall return in a moment:

Putting all these factors together, what we have seen is a most dramatic change in the complexity of systems that can be built and the cost that they can be built for. Engineers are used to talking about this kind of thing in terms of what they refer to as orders of magnitude, a times-ten change. The microelectronics revolution shows a three orders of magnitude change – a thousand to one – in reduction of cost and increase of complexity over only a few years. Nobody knows what the consequences of such a large change will be.

We are historically unfamiliar with changes of this magnitude and it is difficult to identify another. All the way from a man on foot to a modern jet aircraft represents only about two orders of magnitude change in speed of transportation, and that evolution which embraces the whole history of transportation took place over many hundreds of years. In microelectronics we have a three orders of magnitude change taking place over only a decade. There has never been a larger or faster technological revolution in the history of mankind and what we are facing now has justly been compared with the invention of the wheel or the discovery of fire. (Gosling, 1980, 83)

The second step in the revolution involves the storage of information. The development of integrated circuits as part of the search for ever-more sophisticated computing facilities, of itself implies that conventional methods of storing information are rapidly being outmoded. It is already imaginable that an archive of information equivalent to, say, a conventional library of 400,000 volumes, could be available in a device equivalent in size to a 26-inch television receiver, with each item randomly accessible in about one second (Gosling, 1980, 84). Although writing itself, as a communication mode, may not be under threat, the implications for access to information, locally, regionally, nationally, even internationally, are obvious and enormous. The third step in the revolution concerns the transmission of information, communication.

By converting information into inconceivably fleeting pulses of light, it becomes possible to transmit them over vast distances using hair-like fibres of very special glass which trap the light within themselves and carry it almost without loss. Glass, like the silicon of which microcircuits are made, comes from sand — of which there is an inexhaustible supply — and very little goes to make an optical fibre which can carry an enormous flow of information. (Gosling, 1980, 84)

Together the three steps lead us into a society in which the conventional television receiver or monitor becomes a video display unit with enormously enhanced educational potential. The central issue, rightly noted by Gosling, is one to which we shall return at the end of this chapter. For all the firm predictions on these technical changes, some of which are already coming true even earlier than prophesied, nobody knows what the consequences will be in social and economic terms. One of the major reasons for pressing at this juncture for greater freedom to learn and less instruction in our educational system, is that the only certainty for the last part of the twentieth century will be uncertainty: therefore, flexibility and imagination are the qualities we must endeavour to develop in ourselves and our children.

How is the revolution in communication going to affect video? One important facility that has already begun to affect the use of the television receiver is the possibility of access to novel information services such as teletext and viewdata. International usage is tending to suggest that the generic name of an electronic information service in which the information is displayed as 'pages' of text or simple graphics on the screen of a domestic receiver, shall be 'videotex' (Maddison, 1980, 12). This term will therefore increasingly be used to cover an electronic information service, whether it is transmitted as part of the conventional television signal (as 'Ceefax' and 'Oracle' in Britain, 'Qube', 'Viewtron' and others in the USA), or is received as coded telephone signals via a telephone line (as 'Prestel', in Britain). The former of these methods is usually called 'teletext': it offers access to several hundred frames, each displaying up to 24 rows of 40 characters; the viewer at present has to wait up to 50 seconds for any frame he calls up on his keypad, a minor frustration. The second videotex system, originally called 'viewdata' by British Telecom when it was pioneered in the early 1970s, offers access to a much larger data base (currently up to a quarter of a million frames) via the subscriber's telephone and television receiver, together with a special keypad. The system offers almost instant access to any page, but the user is charged not only for the access itself, at a rate set by the provider of the frame, but also his or her own telephone charge, on the standard time basis. These costs, as well as a relatively slow uptake of frame by potential providers, have tended to restrict the attractions of Prestel, although an ingenious development seems to offer not only a wider utilisation but a way of reducing costs for educational users. This is 'telesoftware', a method first devised in 1977, of sending programs from one computer to another, either via broadcast transmission or via the telephone system. By this means a Prestel user, for example, can transfer a program stored on the main computer to his own microcomputer, which will check it for errors and store it on cassette or disc, for later use.

An individual or institution wishing to use Prestel as an information service, and to download telesoftware programs on to a suitable microcomputer, would have to spend (1982 prices) £145 on installation (£265 if a commercial organisation), £268 annual rental and Prestel/

telephone call charges at between approximately 1½p per minute (cheap rate) and 7p per minute (peak rate). Although a 5K program can be captured using this system in only a few minutes, costing around 20p at peak rate, or 9p at cheap rate, so that the comparison with postal charges is already very favourable, the installation and rental charges seem prohibitive for widespread educational use at the time of writing. The former will doubtless fall, but experience suggests that rental charges as well as call rates will rise steadily, unless a deliberate policy to encourage heavy use of the new system is adopted. The Assistant Director of the Council for Educational Technology, which has been the major stimulus to research into the educational potential of Prestel, was understandably eloquent and enthusiastic about the long-term future, when he introduced the first public demonstration of telesoftware, at the annual conference of the Educational Television Association in April 1981 (Willis, 1981, 97-9). As he stressed, the interactive nature of the Prestel system (already permitting certain commercial activities such as ordering a case of wine or booking a holiday abroad — significantly enough!) offers an exciting range of future possibilities compared with the Ceefax/Oracle teletext pages. These are provided and updated for viewing only, although limited interactivity is certainly conceivable, as has been demonstrated in the United States' Qube system, to be discussed below.

To describe the convergence of computing and communication, a whole string of more-or-less hideous new words has been devised. The prize for the most hideous so far should probably go to the term 'compunication', an American usage coined to cover the whole field. 'Computercation', also ugly, would at least retain the stem of 'compute', whereas the other one sounds more like something to do with punishment. The French term 'telematics' has been gaining use in the EEC and is at least briefer than the not very lucid British phrase 'information technology' which was honoured by having 1982 labelled IT year, perhaps in the hope that the citizens of the United Kingdom would be encouraged by the designation of such a strange phrase at least to find out what it meant. 'Telematics: the impact on industry' was the subject of a speech given by the Permanant Secretary of the Department of Industry at the end of February 1981. Sir Peter Carey discussed the implications of telematics for the office, for the stock exchange and the banking world, and for education. The effect on the first area, the office, is the one with which, in addition to industry itself, most of us are familiar, through various television programmes, such as ATV's 'The Mighty Micro' or the BBC's 'Now the Chips Are Down' (1978). It is well known that the video screen will soon become the surface on which we edit texts of letters, update our figures, retrieve documents, using word processors with disc storage rather than paper and filing cabinets. Sir Peter made three useful and relevant points about this revolution of the office: first, every business, however small, has an office – be it a bedsitting room, truck cab or author's study – and the revolution will apply there as well as for ICI; secondly, the current headaches of transition are the greatest we shall face in this process, as new technologies (e.g. direct voice input) are perfected and we humans adapt ourselves; thirdly, the electronic office offers particularly attractive prospects, in terms of speed and cheapness, for the exchange of information. This last point was the salient one for his second area of impact, the world of commerce: here Sir Peter pointed to the fact that the revolution in communications will reduce the significance of traditional geographic centres such as the City or Wall Street, unless they can remain ahead of the field in telematics, offering more swift and cheaper information and communication than rival trading centres. In education, it was encouraging to hear such an influential senior civil servant speaking with emphasis of the urgent need to develop open and continuing education opportunities, and of the salient role of television as an educative force in the society of the future in which 'far less necessary will be the absorption of vast numbers of facts and statistics' (Carey, 1981, 404).

The further development of telematics is seen by governments as an explosively expanding branch of industry. OECD statistics show telecommunications traffic among the 24 industrialised nations growing at 16 per cent annually, at a time when other industrial sectors have been in recession, or slack. In early 1982 it was announced that the giant American Telephone and Telegraph Company would be broken up, to create a 'major international competitor in one of the world's most dynamic industries' (Glynn and Hewitt, 1982, 40). In Britain, the Minister for Information Technology has described his area of responsibility as being 'as economically significant in the 1980s as agriculture was in the last century': British Telecom was separated from the Post Office in Britain at the beginning of this decade.

In addition to the use of the domestic television receiver for videotex, which of itself is likely to have an impact on the amount of conventional broadcasting viewed by the public, the screen will be used for a range of other signals, already available in North America, currently under development for Europe. Between them, videotex, satellite and cable suggest a challenge to the tried and tested European systems for controlling television that looks very difficult to resist; the video market in home computers, cassettes, discs and games, to be discussed in the next chapter, presents a further challenge. There is a problem for society in the very freedom and openness which the new technologies promise. Before considering the communications impact of that promise, let us look briefly at the likely effect of the arrival of satellite and cable television in Europe, both expected before the end of the decade.

Satellites have been used for years to relay television internationally or over major national land masses. Europe has not yet had the opportunity for direct broadcasting by satellite (DBS) mainly because the linguistic and geographic divisions within the continent are so sharp and irregular. Capital expenditures for a satellite system seemed uneconomic, and political imperatives were insufficient to encourage its development. Since the geostationary satellite will be placed in an orbit above the equator, the signal will come from a point only 28° above the horizon in England, less than 20° in North Scotland. Countries with well-established cable networks for television reception (e.g. Belgium — 65 per cent of homes) are much better suited to overcome the technical problems of receiving (and perhaps decoding) a signal from such a low angle above the horizon, since community dish aerials are obviously a useful means of reducing consumer costs (perhaps between £200 and £400 for one's own dish aerial) and environmental clutter. Reception of signals from a satellite directly or via community aerial offers several additional channels with excellent pictures and sound. The estimated (1982) cost of launching, insuring and running a five-channel satellite is at least £175 million. At the time of writing, the questions to be answered about satellite broadcasting are political rather than technical, concerning the financing, control and indeed purpose of this new communications technology (Lowe, 1982a). It has been generally assumed that the major revenue for those who finance the launch and operation of a satellite will come from advertising, perhaps aimed at international audiences. A 1977 agreement stipulates that European satellites should, as far as possible, broadcast to national targets rather than across national boundaries. Current thinking suggests that a major source of revenue to the operators of a satellite will be subscription charges to viewers interested in the additional programming, and higher quality reception (perhaps to include high-quality stereo sound channels) (Lowe, 1982b).

Although satellite broadcasting is one aspect of the explosive forces that are changing television viewing into video usage, there are many question marks about its impact on our society. There can be no doubt about the commercial interest in the new technology: in February 1982, even before arrangements for cable and satellite dissemination of television material (and its control and therefore revenue) had been outlined by the government, three major British firms announced plans to build a satellite to carry not only television but computer data, electronic mail, facsimile and telephone communications (Brooks and Collie, 1982). As Brian Wenham, Controller of BBC2 has pointed out, it is difficult to predict what the current audience will actually want to view by the end of the decade, and what services they will be prepared to pay for directly. He has expressed considerable doubts about the deregulation of broadcasting that is implied by the arrival of satellites and of the sister technology, cable. In the case of cable, as with satellite, if a purely market philosophy is permitted to guide the development of the service, some alarming results may occur. Two satellite channels have already been approved for Britain; others will follow; cable can provide dozens more. The BBC and IBA concern in 1982 was that the new communication technologies might lead to a progressive diminution in choice for those who cannot afford them (as production, talent and funding, and even range of programming, for example, of national sporting events are attracted away to cable contractors) in favour of those who can. It is already recognised that cable networks will concentrate on urban areas and, unless required to extend throughout a community, may be restricted to the 'better end' of a city. Brian Wenham has publicly expressed fears that the satellite and cable technology that underpin his 'Third Age of Broadcasting' could promote social and geographic divisions in Britain, 'unless we can be reassured that Government intends to see that the new opportunities and services will be available to all' (Wenham, 1982).

Why are cable and satellite technologies so intimately connected? There are two major reasons. First, they represent two (related) sources of television images and sound for viewers who currently (in Britain at least) view most of their television via transmissions. To that extent they represent a widening of opportunity for the citizen, on one model, or a dangerous invasion, overwhelming the traditions that have given us the 'best television system in the world'. Secondly, as had been implied already, direct broadcasting by satellite is technically feasible already, but it is a 'wasteful' technology (from the operator's position) in several senses, compared to transmission via satellite to a community cable receiver, especially as cable operators are already supplying signals to many homes in North America and in the rest of Europe. As elsewhere in the worldwide communications industry, the operators of cable networks tend to come from the same professional and commercial-industrial area, or to be the very same people, as those who broadcast television by other means. The pressures on the government to stimulate what has been labelled 'the cabling of Britain' have therefore been very strong from this sector alone, although the value of cable networks for telematics has tended to be stressed by the government itself in explaining the frantic pace at which developments have been proceeding in 1981-2.

The main role of television, according to the Cabinet Office Report of January 1982 'will be the delivery of many information, financial and other services to the home and the joining of businesses and homes by high capacity data links' (Cabinet Office, 1982, para. 1). Yet the Report also acknowledged that the 'initial attraction for home subscribers would be the extra television entertainment channels', and the experimental experience in Britain so far explains why many critics are concerned about the nature of what will be attracting potential subscribers. The Minister for Information Technology, Kenneth Baker, said in March 1982 that he was 'determined that Britain will not just get wall-to-wall Dallas', and his concern was shared by the Minister responsible for broadcasting, but the pace of change and the commercial forces behind are very strong indeed (Brooks, 1982a, 13).

In October 1982, the Hunt Report on cable television in Britain was published. Its recommendations were the subject of a front-page report in a national newspaper a month earlier (Brooks, 1982b) and the detailed leakage, itself confirming informed speculation from many months earlier, gave rise to the accusation of a major broadcasting trade union that the Hunt Committee, instead of considering the social implications of various possibilities and recommending accordingly, had 'done the job the Government required of it' (Fiddick, 1982). The entire public debate on whether Britain required cable television, and if so how it should be administered, had taken less than twelve months; the speed with which the preparatory process had been managed was such as to suggest that further public consultation was likely to be minimal. The Hunt Committee assured the public in its Report that the many social, financial and technical problems raised by critics of the original Information Technology Advisory Panel (ITAP) Report on cable systems could be readily overcome, and urged that approval should be given as soon as possible for the widespread development of cable networks offering up to 30 channels of television material. The vagueness and optimism of the Hunt Report was widely attacked at the time of publication, but the tone and pace of the 'cabling of Britain' had already been set earlier in the year. Although some of the recommendations of the government's ITAP Report were rejected by Hunt, the urgency and vague optimism of the former reappeared in the latter. Why?

As the editor of the *Journal of the International Institute of Communications* bitterly remarked in early 1982, Britain's broadcasting policy 'has not kept pace with the expansion of technological opportunity'. The Annan Report included only 500 words on satellite broadcasting, concluding that 'the general pattern of broadcasting services may need re-examination'. Annan later suggested that 'eventually, governments will have to face the problems of communications policy'. Meanwhile, aggressive commercial forces had leapt in to fill the planning vacuum (Howkins, 1982). As early as April 1982, six months before the Hunt Report was published, the Cabinet Secretary had written to the cable television lobby to confirm that the Government was 'planning to take political decisions' on the go-ahead for expanded cable services. The existing cable television companies were arguing at the time for policies that fitted uncannily closely with the Hunt recommendations. Thus David Hurley, the Chairman of Visionhire, in April 1982, saw three phases to cable expansion:

First we have got to get the existing four channels on our present networks freed from the encumbrance of national programmes. Secondly, we have to develop the networks with new co-axial cables offering 30 to 40 channels. Thirdly, there is the twenty-first century business, of fancy fibre-optic cables and services. (Carson, 1982)

This scenario seems to have been accepted by Hunt, along with the cable companies demand to be freed from supervision by a new quango, or by the IBA.

The hostility with which the Hunt Report was received in some quarters was remarkable. The *Guardian* television critic spoke of 'shameful beginnings', from which cable television would have to be 'rescued' by Parliament. Yet in the absence of a national communications policy and given the economic and technological circumstances of the early 1980s, one can at least understand the urgency with which the information aspects of cable systems had been promoted, and the force of the argument that both cable providers and operators would have to be attracted by relative freedom and the chance of rich profits, for the immense capital investment required to be forthcoming. A government-sponsored report had already suggested that without a vigorous move towards cable systems, Britain's 1981 trade deficit in information technology would grow from £300m to £1,000m annually (Howkins, 1982, 4). The potential for export of both hardware and software was another factor promoting swift decisions, as were the obvious prospects for long-term employment of technical, production and managerial staff to set up, operate and supply the new networks. Nevertheless, doubts remained. It took the best part of 20 years to move from three to four television channels in Britain and arguably the reason for the acknowledged excellence of all four outputs by comparison with television systems in other countries had to do with that same 'lack of choice' some pretended in 1982 to bewail, as well as to the carefully developed arrangements for control (and criticism) that are rightly envied by other societies. Apart from such concerns, all the more significant in their sincerity because of the casual way they appeared to have been brushed aside by the Hunt Committee, it was disappointing to hear no expression of determination to ensure the speediest installation of fibre-optic cables (rather than obsolescent co-axial), a technology in which Britain was reputed to hold a world lead. The most alarming aspect of the whole cable 'debate' in Britain had been the constant reference to transatlantic experience, when enough was already known – particularly in information and cable technology – to have designed a distinctive European cable philosophy to leapfrog rather than ape American systems.

As far as the use of video materials for education and training are concerned, the promise of 30-channel Babel in major conurbations by the late 1980s was as uncertain a prospect as other aspects of cable development. Many could be found in 1982 who regarded the swift advent of avowedly commercial cable television systems, freed from more than the lightest of controls, as an outright disaster. On the other hand the expansion in the general awareness and utilisation of video material of every sort that is implied offers opportunities, it has been argued, for the development of video in education and training, too. Whether educational interests like it or not, cable is coming. The nature of its impact on society and of society's response will be affected at least to an extent by the determination of educational interests and their ingenuity in taking advantage of whatever opportunities may emerge for contribution.

5 VIDEO AT HOME

> The analogy between computers and motor cars is instructive in considering the scale of change: if both industries had developed at the same rate over the past thirty years or so, today a Rolls Royce would cost £1, it would do three million miles to the gallon, and it would deliver enough power to drive an ocean liner. And, if it had been miniaturised, you could get about five hundred on your thumbnail. (Carey, 1981, 402)

From the consumer's point of view, such an effect on the car industry would be both unimaginable and, at first sight, enormously attractive. Only at first sight, perhaps, for we can easily guess the effects of the 'throw-away Rolls' on the car manufacturing industry itself, on our towns, roads and the rest of our battered ecology, as well as the implications of throw-away cars for drivers, passengers and pedestrians. The pace of change in microelectronics is so dramatic that it is impossible to predict which range of devices will emerge as survivors in another decade because factors even more powerful than market forces in the traditional sense will control whether a product is launched, at which price it is sold, how it is marketed, and how long it is available. The result is that the full exploitation of a device by the consumer is very unlikely to occur before a new, more sophisticated and cheaper product appears. Whether or no it is strictly relevant to the perceived needs of the consumer, it may have a brief heyday. This has to an extent been true of certain sectors of the consumer market in the past, but the analogy is with toys or luxury goods, rather than those white goods from which the video consumer's cornucopia is descended. A gloomy view of the future sees society scarred by great disparities between rich and poor, patchy distribution of the blessings (and curses) of the microelectronics revolution, and a chaotic jungle of underemployed hardware littering the floors and dustbins of those houses wealthy enough to continue buying.

This book is partly about this very subject. It is too simple to prophesy either doom or glory; common sense suggests that our future will be mixed and muddled, like our past, but that — perhaps more than before — individual choices will be increased. In this chapter, as well as describing some of the relevant hardware and software currently available and/or predicted for the near future, an attempt will be made to discuss how the consumer may make use of some of the opportunities that are here or about to arrive, and what that may mean for his or her lifestyle. Some of the devices and systems mentioned in the previous chapter will appear here too, but considered from the position of the individual citizen, or group of citizens, in the home. Video itself will be the prime theme, but it will be sensible to look at other areas, especially domestic microcomputers and games, which will play a part in the future of video. Some of the ideas mentioned will be explored further at the end of the book, under the headings of open learning and continuing education.

The growth of the television games industry provides a useful starting point to the discussion. Early versions (still on sale, but with sales only maintained by progressive reductions in price) permitted a single, simple contest (e.g. table tennis) at a fixed pace, in a monochrome format; within a very few years more sophisticated 'games centres' came on the market, offering unlimited scope for the marketing and purchase of new games, sold in cassette form, to be displayed in full colour and played at variable speeds by one or more players. The convergence of these ambitious centres with developments in the home computer market has now been completed, with toy manufacturers offering games centres with computer facilities, while computer manufacturers stress the ability of their latest micro to provide a video games centre. As in other electronic areas, the effect in terms of reduced physical scale and costs has been dramatic. In 1980, Curry's, one of Britain's major electrical appliance retailers, announced their entry into the mini-computer sales area, noting that prices for home computers were coming down from the 'present level of at least £500'. In the summer of 1982 more sophisticated systems than the one or two available in 1980 were on sale in Curry's at a price of between £150 and £200. Rental of these devices (at less than £10 monthly) was further stimulating the demand for them, but the great expansion was predicted for 1983-4, when a revolutionary new generation of microcomputers was expected to enter the arena. Thus far the Japanese impact on microcomputers has been limited and the US industry is awaiting the expected impact with some trepidation, but confidence that the market potential is enormous:

People who say they can't imagine curling up in front of a fire with a computer don't have a very good idea of what computers can look like. We should be able to shove everything into a notebook size computer. Maybe we'll have something that will open up like a book but will be all screen'. (Alan Kay, chief scientist of the Atari Corporation quoted in Marbach *et al*., 1982a, 46)

Meanwhile, related developments proceed rapidly. The effects on television receivers themselves have already been remarkable. In early 1981, a portable monochrome receiver with a 1.5 inch screen was announced by Matsushita Electronics of Osaka. In December 1981, a three-inch colour portable set was being marketed by the same company (at about £230), weighing three pounds, and operating on a rechargeable battery, car cigarette lighter or domestic current, either as a receiver or video unit; six months later the Japanese company Suwa announced the first genuinely flat (monochrome) receiver, based on liquid crystal display technology, to be marketed as a wristwatch (with headphones and lightweight battery pack) in 1983 at under £100 (Abatemarco, 1982a and 1982b). Not all these devices and gadgets will attract buyers; some have little value beyond gimmick attraction; some will be delayed or withdrawn for reasons that will be obscure to all but board members of the corporations that develop them. Returning to the subject of the microcomputer, the development of more powerful microprocessors means that there are already predictions of the arrival (in 1983) of a microcomputer the size of two attache cases, capable of one million instructions per second (i.e. the equivalent of a large business computer), for around £3,000 (perhaps 1 per cent of the conventional machine's cost to a company). Nevertheless, although there is a convergence between traditional computer equipment and usage on the one hand and microcomputing on the other, the apparent gap in costs is exaggerated in this claim (Large, 1982). Although a device with the pure reaction speed and memory store quoted could be built, and even marketed in the near future, two crucial factors will inhibit its progress. First, there is the question of how far such a device can relate to the rest of a family of computers: increasingly it is recognised that individual buyers, like businesses, buy into a range of products rather than an individual device. Secondly, and more significantly, how effective (and expensive in development terms) will be the software and support services for the projected microcomputer? So important have these services become to success or failure of a product that the 1982 prediction of the arrival of such a device seems to have most significance as proving the reality of the old joke that the software is what is for sale and 'we throw in the computer for nothing'.

Whichever video game centre or home computer system attracts the consumer, the explosive expansion of the market for electronic wares implies a worldwide shift in television usage that is already noticeable in some societies. The most marked overall effect is that the screen becomes part of an *interactive* system; primitive though the activity may be at the level of the early video games, the passive viewer has become an active user once the screen is being used to display information that the citizen can call up and affect through his or her actions. Most home computers already offer a simple graphics facility; many critics believe that computer-generated imagery (CGI) offers the most exciting and potentially the most powerful long-term contribution to the usage of domestic video devices. Most of us have seen demonstrations of computer graphics, in broadcast television programmes: a popular sequence might involve the illusion of flying over an artificial landscape, using a joystick to control one's flight path like the pilot of a helicopter or aircraft. Such simulations have been used for some time in initial pilot training. Or an artist may paint freehand on his computer graphics display with an electronic 'brush' in any shade, brightness or hue preferred, which may be adjusted or reworked instantly, as required. The technology at present is confined to very powerful computer systems costing upwards of £200,000 to create: doubtless these will be adapted and marketed at low cost for home computer systems, as part of the revolution that is in progress (Lewell, 1981).

The significance of the video screen in the home will grow swiftly, as the process of convergence continues, the process whereby technologies based on microelectronics borrow and merge their originally separate functions and qualities. Ultimately, some of the devices that have been described will be capable of independent operation, or pooled activity, as well as direct communication with other devices so as to gain access to additional resources (Maddison, 1980, 11). A good example of current possibilities of pooling is offered by a 1981 description of the device called a Microwriter, a portable system permitting the user to write copy straight into type, to be tidied up afterwards on the office's word processor. The device, as described in 1981, only had a single-line display of 12 characters, so that the author's ability to check text was impeded when copy had to be reviewed on the Microwriter itself. A much more convenient resource was to be found at home:

> If I connect it through an interface box to my domestic television set, it displays the text as I go (complete with moving cursor) and I can alter the layout as I plan it. My sitting-room 'tele' has become a

display screen for a word processing system: a tool as personal to me as the pad of paper on which I also, from time to time, record my personal thoughts. (Willis, 1981, 99)

Already, a year later, a new generation of 'travel computers' has overtaken this usage. Convergence is again displayed in the 1982 description of a device measuring 3 x 13 x 10 inches, with a 128K character memory (using 'bubble' circuits, which do not erase data when switched off, so that no separate disc or tape store is required), powered by battery and offering a flip-up screen that displays up to four lines of writing. The computer can be operated independently, connected via telephone to the office (or home) computer, or used as a portable word processor. The launch price was just over £1,200 (Abatemarco, 1982b, 3). An even more impressive device was announced in August 1982, a revolutionary computer (with a six-inch flip-up display screen) that fits easily into half the volume of a standard briefcase. Not only does this device have a 'bubble' memory of greater capacity than desk-top computers five times in size, but its software is delivered over telephone lines from the company's mainframe computer. The Grid Compass, as it is called, can also send or receive information from other databases – news, stock market quotations, bookings for hotels, purchases or graphic displays to support or illustrate a salesman user's demonstration. It is predicted by some that the portable computer will eventually become the standard personal instrument, although the present price tag on the Grid Compass (approximately £3,700) is in the executive bracket rather than that of the home user (Marbach *et al.*, 1982b).

The videodisc is an item of hardware born in a controversy that may yet turn out to be more important than the hardware itself. The controversy stems from dispute over whether the system, which is independent of any videocassette replay system, will sell to the consumer. For the home video user, on the one hand, videodisc offers considerably enhanced qualities of sound and vision reproduction, precise access to individual frames, great durability, and other possibilities referred to below. On the other hand, videodiscs were launched in 1980 in the USA in three rival (incompatible) formats and have not sold particularly well, probably because of their obvious drawbacks. The user has to buy a player dedicated to the products of the manufacturer (it cannot play other material, or record material of the user's own choice, so that wiping or editing existing material is impossible, under present technology). The storage space required for disc material is much greater than that required for existing videocassettes. Although Philips announced in June 1982 the launch in Britain of their laservision version of videodisc, some critics had already declared that disc was doomed, since within another two years the launch by five leading manufacturers, including Philips, of the new (compatible) 8mm cassette format would offer comparable picture and sound quality and a miniature one-piece camera/recorder system that would attract strong consumer support (Kirk, 1982a). The epitaph may be premature. Although the British launch of the laservision hardware has understandably been accompanied by the release of a catalogue carrying over 100 entertainment titles, half of them feature films, the element that is most likely to save videodisc from death is its interactivity. Even if the system itself dies, the principle of interactivity will certainly re-emerge in other forms in the home video experience and video producers will have learned from the videodisc of the enormously wider range of usages now opening up for the user, if suitable material is prepared.

The significance of the videodisc for the home user stems from three remarkable qualities — the precision with which individual frames can be accessed, the speed with which this random access can be achieved, and the possibility, dependent on these two features, of coupling the system to a microcomputer so that attractive home video education and training opportunities of a truly flexible nature can be devised. The astonishing speed of random access in the disc systems, together with the ability to run the machine at a range of speeds, slower or faster than real time while maintaining perfect picture quality and synchronous sound, will presumably become a standard feature of many formats of home video in the next few years. It implies a new 'grammar' for television production, since the user can supply, for example, 'slow motion replay' of an event or create a 'time-lapse photographic record' of another, on his or her own initiative or as suggested by the video material itself or by support materials supplied with it. Precise random access means that the videodisc is the first video system that can truly be compared to a book, from the user's point of view.

> The indexing system on a videodisc is divided into chapters and can then be further sub-divided into seconds, tracks or frames (depending on the system), which are analogous to the book's chapters, pages or paragraphs. The access mechanisms of discs and books are similar in that they can be accessed by the chapter, or browsed through in slow or fast searches, or skimmed, or studied slowly, or repeated as often as required by the user. (Turner and Mackenzie, 1982, 5)

Not only does the videodisc (and new forms of home video to follow) have the advantage over the book of colour and movement for real events or animated diagrams, but it can also be readily linked to a home computer, which can itself only generate relatively crude graphics, colour and sound. The computer can then be used both to control the disc and to respond to the user's commands, perhaps stimulated by viewing the disc material. In other words, the true significance of the disc, or of other devices that may offer similar high-speed random access to individual frames, is not its high-quality reproduction of vision and sound, but its interactivity, the fact that it is controlled by the user. One videodisc already in production will contain hundreds of frames reproducing still pictures of paintings (some never before on public display) from major galleries; other areas of the disc will include a documentary-style illustrated commentary, pages of printed text and notes for reading biographical information on the artists and details of the galleries; throughout the disc optional caption sequences and alternative soundtracks will permit different levels of study. The encylopaedia *Joy of Knowledge* was planned from the start to integrate with discs to be published at a later stage and utilised in a similar manner (Chittock, 1981, 169).

To most citizens in Britain, the phrase 'video at home' will conjure up the image of the videocassette recorder that has had such an impact on the British television industry in the past few years. In 1982 the video recorder market in Britain was actually greater than that for the USA and moving towards the size of the Japanese market, despite the higher living standards and much larger populations of both countries. The phenomenal growth of video usage in Britain was fuelled by the unusual British tradition of rental, which accounted for over 60 per cent of the sales of new recorders in 1982, and the fact that a substantial portion of the usage was by working-class viewers. There are some curious commercial side-effects of the extraordinary size of the British videocassette recorder market, which can best be understood by considering the purposes for which the recorders are bought or rented. The first use, not possible on the videodisc systems, has always been the illegal off-air recording of broadcast material, especially feature films. This is still a dominant (86 per cent) element in the usage which a sample of owners and renters was making in late 1981: they watched approximately four and a half hours weekly. The British market for blank videocassettes should top 80 million in the year 1985-6, and at least one publisher was planning in 1982 to take advantage of these enormous sales by offering cassettes carrying 'watch and wipe' magazines of sport, travel and interviews at a figure set within the standard price bracket for different types of *blank* cassettes: naturally the magazines were planned to be punctuated by advertisement spots (Kleinman, 1982). One of the biggest British entertainment industry interests (Thorn-EMI) was spending over £3 million annually in 1982 and planned more for 1983, on programming for cassettes to buy or hire ready-made. At first, most of this part of the video market was absorbed by copies of feature films, which in 1981 were selling far better than had been predicted, and by pornography and violence of various kinds. Clearly, influential manufacturers expect this pattern to change.

Two medium-term social effects of the immense success of video recorder sales in Britain may be that the style of cable television will not reflect the American experience as closely as has been predicted by some, and that the spread of videotex (and perhaps other video resources) into British homes may be less extensive and swift than in some other societies. In an attempt to stimulate interest in Prestel, a pilot scheme was launched in 1982 to instal one of the special jack-plugs offering access to the system, in each of 100,000 selected homes, free of charge. It was argued that this would encourage awareness and utilisation of Prestel, a technology in which Britain was at the time leading the world (McRae, 1982). National videotex systems are under development in other countries, but Britain was the first to open a full public service, in 1979. The experimental cable systems hurriedly set up in Britain from late 1981 reflected the shape of the videocassette recorder market as well as taking account of the very extensive North American cable television experience. The cable industry in the United States is enormous and growing fast: two separate activities are involved; the provision and operation of a cable system and the creation, or at least purchase and supply of, material to the operators. Charges for connection of a house to a cable system are low (approximately £5 monthly in 1981) and subscribers near a conurbation such as New York may receive 20 'free' channels, and live coverage of the House of Representatives; several local channels are also provided, as agreed by the operators when contracting with civic authorities for the franchise. In addition, a graduated scale of charges offers optional access to special channels showing films or sports or children's programmes and so forth. Apart from this pattern of provision, Warner-Amex operate in Columbus, Ohio, the famous cable operation called Qube, which some see as a signpost to future cable systems. This celebrated interactive system offers viewers the opportunity to 'vote' with their keypads when invited in the cabled programme and to see displayed at once the percentage division of their views on the subject. As has been pointed out, although the operation is claimed as ultimate, instant democracy, Qube offers commerce and industry a potentially invaluable opportunity to sample tastes and preferences on aspects of life traditionally investigated at great expense and length by advertising agencies (Rowley, 1981, 6-9). The potential for other less sinister purposes (e.g. views on aspects of local government or piloting of new programme ideas) is also very considerable and certainly affords another example of the new technology's challenge to conventional models of broadcasting.

From the view of the urban citizen of 1982, cable, if not already available, offers a great extension of television sound and images, but all the evidence suggests that the actual consumption of this rich menu must be very low. This is not only a statement of the obvious fact that no person, however fish-eyed, can watch more than one or two channels out of 20, at once. It is also a reflection of the downgrading of purposeful television viewing as an activity. All of the first five cable television operators in Britain grumbled in 1982 about their customers telephoning to complain about the number of repeats on their new channel, which in every case was almost exclusively showing feature films. 'You don't have to reschedule your life to catch a film now. With cable you can watch it at another, more convenient time.' The converse of this is that the cable user is not expected to sit down to watch a single channel every night for several hours: the very idea is ludicrous to a North American viewer, but in Britain the small number of cable channels available in 1982 was responsible for the complaints quoted (Francis, 1982, 28).

Despite the possibilities for 'answering back' implied by Qube, the cable industry is financially supported, administered and supplied in ways that are familiar from the world of broadcasting. To that extent, it has comparatively little to do with the revolution implied by the arrival of video in the broader sense in the home. Even Qube, as has been mentioned, is financed and operated by a massive communications organisation mainly for its own interests: it is arguably a manipulative device of great sophistication compared to earlier systems of audience and consumer research, but still a manipulative device. The main theme of this chapter, and indeed of this book, concerns the actions of individual video users rather than the reception (even with the option of 'answering back') of television by large audiences. Much more significant than the spread of cable systems for the future of video at home will be the development of specially made material, whether in cassette or disc or later formats for use by the individual at his or her own pace.

Thorn-EMI, mentioned earlier as having a major commitment to programming, plan in their first wave of production, not only entertainment material (ranging from classical recitals to spectacular rock groups) but, intriguingly, courses on car maintenance and dress-making (Stringer, 1982). Other producers are creating video language courses and direct teaching for a great range of ages, aptitudes and interests: the titles outlined so far are hardly very imaginative but the market (rental and indeed public library assisting, as well as direct sales) will doubtless provide plenty of stimulus in time.

What are the real prospects of video at home becoming a key aspect of a revolution in communication and education? The idea of an active learner utilising several resources from the converging technologies in an interactive fashion is imaginable, but will it happen? The stimuli towards such a development are plain enough. The new devices are going to offer increasing opportunities for interactive learning and access to larger databases than most homes have possessed: the fact that they will do so is already an important weapon in the marketing of the devices themselves. As Gosling has pointed out, there is a positive incentive to manufacturers to design and produce more complex versions of microelectronic devices because the increased complexity of a specific chip's layout does not of itself increase the cost of its manufacture. Three factors militate against the revolution stimulating successfully the arrival of the active learner. The cost of hiring or buying electronic devices, although still falling, must reach a plateau in real terms because of the need to recover research and development costs, marketing costs and indeed the manufacturing costs of the mechanical and casing elements of the device being sold. Although a device may be available at 'only £10 monthly', that sort of sum will be beyond the spending power of members of society most able to benefit from the revolution, those with time on their hands and strong motives to find new skills or new outlets for their existing skills – the unemployed. Secondly, although motivation towards active learning may be strong in a society in which the work ethic is a paramount value, will that still be true in a society affected by structural unemployment, a society sometimes called 'post-industrial'? Will not the attractions of entertainment far outweigh those of education and training? Finally, can education and training adapt to provide materials that will be sufficiently attractive to the active learner to continue to stimulate him or her after initial enthusiasm has waned or obstacles have been met? This is primarily a question about the approach to education itself. It has been discussed already and will be the subject of the last part of this book.

The first obstacle — cost — may prove to be of less significance than it seems at present. Even for Third World citizens, the true poor of our planet, the progressive miniaturisation, increased performance, falling power consumption and real costs of the devices must mean that they will swiftly begin to be accessible, at first only to the city-dweller and the minority with a wealthy life-style, eventually to wider groups. It should not be forgotten that governments have a considerable incentive to spread the use of microelectronic devices, so as to release manpower for tasks that cannot be handled by the machines and particularly to create realistic opportunities for education and training on a large scale. Therefore the individual active learner should find that government action as well as industrial market forces will work in harmony with the nature of the technology itself to make educational opportunities more accessible. Devices might be installed in communities to provide or stimulate awareness and basic skills; personalised equipment might follow at a later stage. This factor, the possibility of government intervention to stimulate usage of microelectronics, has already been at work in Europe and it is likely to continue to have a positive effect on the two other obstacles mentioned — the question-mark over learner motivation in a society with high permanent unemployment, and the danger that a national educational system itself may prove incapable of adapting itself to cope with the new challenges posed. In Britain, the Microelectronics Education Programme that is intended to ensure that every secondary school shall have at least one microcomputer has cost over £9 million at a time when the government in power has elsewhere doggedly stuck to a policy of reduced public expenditure, particularly in education. An important additional factor must be that children themselves, as discussed in the next chapter, are experiencing more rapid and marked changes in their learning environment than other groups. As they grow up and enter either the world of work or, more likely, occasional project work interspersed with long periods where they will be able to plan their own time, their experience will make them much more aware than our generation of the educational scope of video at home.

In the long term, therefore, there is little doubt about the transformations that are likely to occur. Some experiments with interactive video are already in production. Sony have already developed their Video Responder system, linking the domestic video receiver to a Sony U-Matic videocassette recorder via a 'student unit', an A4-size pad equipped with ten buttons and a retaining clip to hold work-sheets or notes. The student inserts a specially prepared videocassette: the first segment having been viewed, the student is asked (on the screen) to select one of, say, six responses to a question designed to test understanding of the first segment. If the wrong response is selected on the set of buttons, the display politely tells the student so and invites a second try or (as programmed) rewinds automatically to show the first segment. If the correct response is selected, or correct digits (perhaps in answer to a question requiring calculations) are typed into the unit, the second segment follows. At the end of the learning sequence, the student is automatically informed of his or her score, and the time taken to select each response is also recorded. The system is an impressive attempt to make fuller use of obsolescent technology and is particularly aimed at the training needs of industry and public services (many organisations having already bought U-Matic machines) offering individual pacing and detailed information on individual accuracy and speed of progress through the material. There is no doubt that Sony will itself outmode the Video Responder within a few years, but their ingenious system, despite its relative crudeness compared to what will follow, combines the merits of pioneering with sensible use of equipment already widely available. Their concentration on individual learning, and also the emphasis on the ability of the teacher to modify existing videocassettes into Responder form, are pointers to ways in which education is already changing. The weaknesses of the system, discussed in Chapter 1 above (limited and delayed access to the video material, and restriction of responses to simple programmed learning style) will both disappear in the technological improvements confidently predicted within the decade. The weakness of the way the system has been developed, derived as it is from traditional educational models, teacher-centred, and didactic, is another matter.

Again and again, consideration of the most promising and powerful applications of video in association with new technology draws one towards the same theme, the essential need to recognise that the video revolution implies a challenge to traditional models of education. Broadcast television itself, as has also been discussed, traditionally shares with education the 'banking concept' of knowledge, whereby knowledge is regarded as 'a gift bestowed by those who consider themselves knowledgeable upon those whom they consider know nothing' (Freire, 1968, quoted in Dallos, 1980, 39). As has already been remarked, Socrates, one of the greatest teachers our world remembers, regarded himself not as knowledgeable but as ignorant, a view consistent with his development of the dialectic method of discussion. This involved devising questions to which simple answers had to be framed, unwitting precursors of the computing 'bit' of knowledge that forms the basic unit of information in data processing systems. This 'bit' (an acronym for 'binary digit') is the digit 0 or 1 which may be readily encoded as 'yes' or 'no'. Socrates, just like the computer programmer, aimed always to ask questions that could be answered by 'yes' or 'no'.

The industrialised world has become so familiar with television in its homes that few children would draw a living room without a 'box' in the corner, and indeed any of our citizens with time to spare (young, elderly, unemployed) already make heavy use of that box. In the current decade the tendency for each child to regard the box in the corner as his or her own (as described in the next chapter) will grow, and its enhanced value as a video device rather than as a mere receiver will give it even more potential for good or ill in home life. This chapter has tried to suggest that in so far as the effects will tend towards greater individual independence and power, they will form part of a broader movement towards activity rather than passivity in response to video material, a welcome trend that Socrates would have approved.

6 VIDEO IN THE SCHOOL

In 1979, the headmistress of a Suffolk school asked a group of 22 children aged between 8 and 11 to write down in 15 minutes the titles of all the television programmes they liked. Between them they named 242 programmes, many of which they had not seen for some time. Of the titles in that list only one was a schools television programme. In this chapter the charm and power of broadcast television at home will be contrasted with the relative weakness of most broadcast educational television material, at least in most British schools and at least at present. The likelihood that this comparison will be less marked in another few years from now is discussed, as new roles are found for video in the school. A notable long-term result seems to be a lowering of traditional barriers between schools and the community, and between educators and the creators of educational video material, as co-operative ventures become more common, and more rewarding. The headmistress mentioned above, Gwen Dunn, spent a year observing children aged four and younger and their use of television, for the Independent Broadcasting Authority. Her observations led her to publish the assessment that children under five years old are among the heaviest television viewers in Britain; her recommendations to the families that permit, indeed encourage, that level of viewing included the interesting and strongly stated view that passive, silent viewing should be leavened as far and as frequently as possible by discussion and explanation among the family, of the material being viewed (Dunn, 1977).

In a paper delivered to the Educational Television Association in 1979, Gwen Dunn returned again to the point that both schools and parents take inadequate account of the enormous influence television already has on the lives of children from infancy to the age of adolescent (and, she might have added, beyond). She made several suggestions for the Association to consider promoting, all concerned with trying to alter the curious attitude of those in authority to the power of 'the box in the corner'.

> First and paramount I'd like to see everybody — every single individual concerned with education — accept the fact that television has been invented . . . It's no good nursery schools, infant schools and

those who train teachers to work in them, saying, 'they get enough of that at home', and trying to ignore television. Television won't go away. It's time it was given its wedding ring and a crisp veil and married to the respectable body of education. And in the next HMI's report, I'd like to see a lot about it and in the next enormous Annan Report I'd like to see more than eight or nine papers on what was labelled 'education'. (Dunn, 1980, 51)

Secondly, Gwen Dunn suggested that much more should be done to inform children (and indeed parents and teachers) by first-hand experience about what television is, how it is produced (and she might have added, 'funded, planned and distributed', as far as older children are concerned), so that they may begin to develop critical powers and exercise greater choice over their use of its products. She might have added that such experience should be particularly valuable as cable and other technical developments begin to open up access to a wider range of products for consumption and also access to individuals and groups for creating video themselves for others.

The amount of viewing on the part of children is not only greater in volume than most schools acknowledged, even in 1982; it is different in nature. The A.C. Nielsen Company compiles data on viewing patterns (principally for broadcasters and advertisers) that provide evidence on American children's behaviour that would startle many teachers. For example, it is not surprising that half the average weekly viewing of American children under 12 takes place between 4.30 p.m. and 11 p.m., although it is noteworthy that the children's own programmes shown in the day at weekends are less heavily viewed than prime-time material. It may surprise some that 33 per cent of all average weekly viewing for children between 6 and 11 takes place between 8 p.m. and 11 p.m.; even for children aged 2 to 5, the biggest slice of viewing (22 per cent of the total) takes place in that period. At 11 p.m., 10 per cent of all 6 to 11-year olds still form part of the total audience (Nielsen Co., 1979; quoted in Adler *et al.* 1980, 18-19). The average child under 12 in America spends approximately 27 hours per week watching television. An interesting result is that it has been calculated that the average high-school graduate has passed some 22,000 hours of his or her life (or well over six years of 365 eight-hour days, rather more time than is spent in school) in front of the set. He or she may have been exposed to as many as 350,000 commercial messages in that time (Adler *et al.*, 1980, 1). Similar calculations can no doubt be made for the young of European or Japanese families. While the association between the viewing of violence on television remains a subject of considerable interest to authority and to research workers, little attention has been paid to much more pervasive and repetitive influences such as commercials and, indeed, of 'conspicuous consumption' in typical television drama and films, on the moral development of children (or for that matter the effects on families as a whole).

In view of the heavy proportion of children's viewing time taken up by programmes *not* specifically designed for them, there is perhaps an element of irony in the close control that has traditionally been exercised over the content and style of children's programmes. In the early 1970s, the Children's Television Workshop based in New York commissioned a series of very expensive research studies from which emerged 'Sesame Street'. This series of educational programmes was intended to transform literacy and numeracy among preschool children. It uses similar devices to those of the producers of commercial advertisements to attract and retain children's attention: loud noises, bouncy music, friendly monster puppets, and so on. The Workshop, despite the advice of some of their own consultants, assumed that if the style was attractive to preschool children, the content (adult jokes and rote learning of numbers and letters) would be intelligible. Despite early successes, this has not been as dramatically borne out as was predicted. It is perhaps significant that an off-shoot of 'Sesame Street', 'The Muppet Show', retaining all but the rote learning (the original major purpose) has since become a popular prime-time programme (Noble, 1975, 96).

In Britain, the swift spread of videocassette recorders to schools as well as homes has had important effects on the utilisation of broadcasting designed specifically for school audiences. In 1980, the Head of BBC Schools Television reported that 86 per cent of secondary schools possessed one or more recorders, an increase of 16 per cent over 1978. 'Of our series for 13 to 18-year olds, 90-95 per cent of the use is in recorded form, and secondary schools have, on average, 74 hours of recorded television material in their libraries' (reported by O'Grady, 1980). Even among primary schools, the proportion with one or more video recorders had increased from 7 per cent in 1978 to 12 per cent by 1980, and no doubt has advanced further since. This trend not only mirrors the spread of these devices in the wider society; it also reflects the very considerable advantages they offer to teacher and to learners, in terms of utilisation of video material, traditionally delivered by transmission. In the long term, the larger schools will increase their holdings of video material, which will come not only from commercial and educational sources but through their own activity. As the video market continues to expand, co-operation over the creation of learning materials by the various producers will tend to increase. Signs of this already began to be noticeable in 1982. The BBC microelectronics project of 1982-3, involves not only the production of two series of programmes to be transmitted on Sunday mornings (i.e. for those who already have an interest in the subject). It is also supported by a device developed by Acorn and marketed as 'The BBC Microcomputer', as well as by a course on programming and by information on local clubs and courses organised with the help of educational authorities. A special videocassette was created for the BBC and Acorn by a university educational television unit for use in in-service teacher training centres. It is intended that software for the computer will be available via telesoftware, utilising the Ceefax teletext system.

Although the example of co-operation described was over a project designed by BBC Continuing Education primarily for adults, it exemplifies an approach to curricular planning and the creation of study materials that fits the needs of schools for video material over the next few years. The arrival of microcomputers in schools has far greater significance for education generally than merely offering a new aspect of mathematical study. In Minnesota, the Education Computing Consortium has purchased more than 5,000 personal computers for use in elementary and high schools and has begun to create (and sell) its own educational software (Marbach *et al.*, 1982a, 46). The director of the consortium tells the story of a blizzard closing a Minnesota school at lunchtime in the winter of 1981-2, so that all the children left for home within minutes, except for those in the computer classroom who refused to leave. The fascination of the microcomputer for most young children derives not only from its novelty, but also from its endless patience; the young also possess both the time and persistence required to create one's own programs. Adults tend to find both these characteristics frustrating.

Indeed, while the transformations in the school implied by the video revolution may cause problems for certain teaching staff, children are unlikely to find any difficulties with an increase in video materials for study, any more than with computer-based learning. Therefore, a key element in the microelectronics education programme in Britain, and in similar movements elsewhere, is the in-service training of teachers. The pace of change, as well as its radical nature, means that the inadequacy of in-service training programmes in many affected industries is already the most serious obstacle to effective utilisation of the new technology.

Nowhere is this more true than in the education industry, where imagination is at a premium. Yet the tradition in teaching has lent great authority to experience and in particular has suggested that a teacher, once trained, needs no further re-education or retraining to orient him or her to new ideas. The need for this view to be reconsidered is great indeed at this moment, if we are on the edge of what Professor Gosling has called a technological abyss, the other side of which is like a foreign land. If the only thing about the future of which we can be sure is that it will surprise us, we can also be sure that our need to prepare to retrain those responsible for schools and students to take account of that is urgent and great.

Video materials themselves, controlled perhaps by microcomputers, would offer a peculiarly appropriate method of solving the problem of how to cope with the unprecedented need to retrain teachers. In case the point has not been taken, the problem is not that teachers need to add to their armoury of skills, but rather that they need to be made aware of the social, economic and educational implications of the revolution that is upon us and to apply their understanding of them to their own subject. The reasons for suggesting that video materials would be singularly appropriate to play a central role in the process of training include the obvious point that the training can by this means be designed to include examples of applications relevant to a specific part of the curriculum and to a specific age group. In addition, the training modules, if prepared imaginatively, could embody the requirement that, as part of their reorientation, teachers should redesign an aspect of their course, or rather of their students' course (a significant alteration), utilising an approach akin to the training they have undergone. As a practical suggestion, the adaptation of the Open University's ingenious 'self-instructional guide to the writing of self-instructional materials' to a video format and for a lower (primary or secondary school) level of student would offer a valuable start to designing a suitable training course (Rowntree and Connors, 1979).

The reorientation required is important because some of the bases on which all schooling has hitherto rested are among the elements likely to be affected by the revolution. For example, if unemployment is to become as widespread and as structural as many predict, the idea that school must involve a preparation for the world of work as traditionally understood is in question. If so, mute acceptance of the authority of seniors and teachers becomes less important than self-reliance, which many would claim has always been more important in any case. Co-operative endeavour to manage projects and solve common problems becomes a much more important element in preparing children for the world they will face, than skills of passing examinations or doggedly learning lumps of information to be regurgitated in written form. There is dispute about the long-term effects on employment of the microprocessor. One of the most influential pessimistic judgements has come from two officials of one of Britain's larger trades unions, who in 1979 wrote a widely quoted book called *The Collapse of Work*. In it, the argument is developed that although work may be a psychological need for healthy human beings, it is only economically necessary during the process of industrialisation. The schools are seen as key areas for altering attitudes, although trades unions and politicians are also criticised for discussing unemployment as something that can and will disappear in the developed world. They might usefully have added that, of course, full employment has never been the experience of Third World countries: it may be that psychologically the North has something to learn from the South on this subject. The book argues that the new technology further increases the costs of labour, while encouraging attractive economies of scale that imply that 'it is now in the interests of capitalists to *disemploy* people if profits are to be made' (Jenkins and Sherman, 1979).

Not every economist or politician believes that microtechnology means the collapse of employment, but all surely accept that there are bound to be massive changes in the patterns of employment, and that change rather than stability will become the hallmark of the adult employment experience in years to come. In this case the traditionally respected schooling qualities of hard work, acceptance of routine and discipline, and a respectful, respectable attitude to authority, lose much of their value. Careers guidance became relatively important in Western schools activity, as full employment declined in the late 1970s. Whatever the precise pattern of employment to be expected in the next decade or so, it is likely to be the case that the minority entering an assured professional career will dwindle further, and that guidance will be more valuable for the majority of school-leavers if it concentrates on the development of lifeskills. All members of the teaching profession need to reconsider their approach to current responsibilities and areas of expertise. Being a worker is only one of a number of roles that may be filled at various times in one's life, and the school experience ought to prepare our young as effectively as possible to fulfil these roles. The American psychologists, Donald Super and J.A. Bowlesbey, define the various life roles as follows:

Child — a role that may last well beyond legal maturity, as long as parents survive.

Student — likely in future to last well beyond youth and to be very important at times in adult life.

Worker — a major life-role for most, but subject to change and unlikely to be continuous to age 60.

Spouse — even outside marriage, being involved in a long-term relationship will be a very significant commitment for almost everyone.

Parent — a role that requires skill and demands energy and stamina as well as love.

Citizen — a role that is likely to become more important, especially at community level, in a post-industrial society.

Leisure — also likely to become more important, so that the management of one's free time becomes an important skill.

Homemaker — a role to be adopted once an individual leaves the parental home.

(Super and Bowlesbey, 1979)

To these roles, the British organisers of the Counselling and Careers Development Unit based at Leeds University add two more:

Consumer — a major role that can be disastrous if mishandled, especially as variable income implies differing spending powers at different periods.

Friend — a difficult role that involves time and energy.

(Scally and Hopson, 1981)

Of course, the giving of information, the teaching of many basic subjects, must continue as a major part of school life. But if more social instability, more choice, more ambiguity, fewer certainties, are to be expected, the emphasis should shift away from the banking of knowledge (which in any case will be one of the areas transformed by the development of new databases and of better and swifter access to them) towards the acquisition of skills. The Leeds team had developed teaching programmes by 1980 on several topics including 'how to communicate effectively', 'how to make, maintain and end relationships', 'how to manage time effectively', and so on (Hopson and Scally, 1980). One is not suggesting that training in acquisition of these lifeskills should replace the bulk of conventional academic study. Rather, just as development of lifeskills seems likely to become much more important in the work of the careers teacher, so emphasis in academic subjects could and should shift in a parallel fashion. For example, in my own original academic subject, history, the conventional approach is to regard the role of the professional historian as a long-term aim for a minority of highly talented students, preceded by careful study at school of large amounts of historical narrative, critical writing and practice in commenting on that criticism. To allow for the influence of a 'lifeskills' approach to school would be to acknowledge that understanding and engaging in the role of historian is itself a skill that many may need and use in later life. Every citizen could and should understand something of international history, so as to exercise judgements on news reports of international issues. Children and parents with understanding of the skills of local history can expect to have both the time and the ability to access appropriate records to be able to use some of those skills. The abilities to seek out evidence, interpret and criticise it and then communicate judgements upon it (the skills of a professional historian) are skills with transfer value to other roles. Approaching the study of history in this way is already a standard procedure in some schools, but it is barely reflected in examination syllabi as yet, nor in the way in which certification itself is managed. There is still an enormous emphasis on the ability to absorb and repeat, in written form, large amounts of information, an emphasis that is entirely inappropriate for the needs of a society in which access to information will be easier, as will its reorganisation and recall, and in which the writing of essays and reports will surely dwindle in importance.

In the first chapter of this book, reference was made to the Schools Council Project on Communication and Social Skills. In this two-year experiment, secondary-school teachers of a wide range of academic subjects were persuaded to involve groups of pupils in the creation of audio-visual teaching materials on aspects of the curriculum. The most striking effects of the projects on the children involved, especially those regarded as of lower academic ability, were a growth in their motivation, an improvement in self-concept, and a marked growth in their use of a wide range of language and communication skills (Lorac and Weiss, 1981, 121-45). Whereas writing, like the use of the microcomputer, is an individual, introverted activity, there are four aspects of producing audio-visual communications that differentiate it (Lorac and Weiss, 1981, 161). First, the collaborative nature of the process, particularly where video is the selected medium, implies social roles and relationships that may not emerge in a conventional classroom. A child that is not very capable by standard academic measures may have particular skills in video presentation, expertise in the subject chosen or in managing the rest of the group, that stimulate skilful and precise use of language, as well as working, as one teacher put it 'in a co-ordinated way for a common goal'. Drama work might be said to stimulate similar skills, but drama does not have the merit of being directed to any aspect of the academic curriculum, a key feature of the project described. The second remarkable feature for pupils of creating audio-visual statements about an academic topic is that it implies a relative comprehensiveness of approach, compared to writing; it may utilise illustrations, diagrams, dramatic reconstructions, scenes recorded on site, sounds, music, even writing itself. Thirdly, the artefact, unlike a written essay, becomes a relatively public statement on completion, for exposure to large groups of other children (and teachers) and, if successful, probably for retention in the school's audio-visual library as a future study resource. Finally, the social relevance of audio-visual media, especially video, is obvious in a world in which already the average child spends more time watching television than attending school (Lorac and Weiss, 1981, 162-74).

The Microelectronics Education Programme is a misnomer. Its intention and effect is to introduce students and teachers to the capabilities and resources of a microcomputer. That is a worthy and urgent aim. One unintended result of greater dependence on microcomputers at school and at home, especially as video will remain at least as salient in the child's world of the next 20 years, may be to encourage introversion and to reduce communication and social skills. Since the latter do not feature as important elements in conventional curricula, the work of the Schools Council Project suggests a very valuable means of increasing both student motivation and understanding of academic subjects, while stimulating that command of certain lifeskills hitherto neglected, yet of great importance in school experience. Greater leisure time, probably lower standards of living for the majority, and an uncertain work future: these predictable implications should be at least as much the concern of a genuine microelectronics education programme as computer literacy. Perbaps the most significant aspect of the four characteristics of audio-visual creativity mentioned by Lorac and Weiss is the co-operative or collaborative nature of the process. To redress the balance tilted by the introspective experiences of viewing video material and studying or programming computerised materials, collaborative endeavours should be an even more significant element in educational activity at schools than hitherto. Many primary and secondary schools lay a certain emphasis on such activities already, especially in non-academic areas of the curriculum. The emphasis ought to spread to academic subjects also, and the creation of relevant video materials suggests a valuable and increasingly accessible means to do so. As changes continue in our society, the tendency to regard the local school as a community resource (for entire families to utilise in the evenings, for example) is a healthy trend that shrewd principals will encourage. Collaborative audio-visual projects for the benefit of wider educational and even social purposes than a particular curricular topic can be imagined, and could contribute strongly to community purposes, perhaps via local or regional cable television.

7 VIDEO IN FURTHER AND HIGHER EDUCATION

Some of those responsible for education in primary or secondary schools may have found some of what was said in the previous chapter irritating, since it may have seemed to ignore the fact that there is no doubt that British schools have undergone more changes of role, personnel and style than other educational institutions in the past 30 years. I wrote earlier of the vivid contrast between a particular secondary modern schoolteacher's determination to instil discipline, by physical force if necessary, and the fact that the pupils concerned were about to leave school for ever. I might have added that the school itself was about to be transformed from a selective (lower intellectual potential) school to a 'comprehensive' (non-selective) institution. The staff's ability to declare ignorance of such an important event or total hostility towards it was impressive evidence of the ability of a group to digest or deflect administrative changes that the public were being told would transform the institutions affected. I cannot say, from first-hand knowledge at least, how successful the staff were, but there is no doubt that those changes were expected to alter secondary education in Britain in a radical way: resistance or apathy among key staff must have been a factor in disappointment that has followed. Nothing so dramatic has occurred in tertiary education over the same period and indeed, as far as television is concerned, further and higher education has continued without its traditional ways of working being altered very much at all. With proper caution, then, we can explore in this section the likelihood that transformations may be expected in post-compulsory education, not only in Britain but around the world over the next few years.

In 1979, the Council for Educational Technology, the body that advises the Department of Education and Science on the promotion and application of educational technology, produced a pamphlet on the contribution of new methods to higher education in the 1990s (CET, 1979). In it the Council referred to the considerable provision already made by higher education for educational technology applications, by the establishment of central facilities such as were discussed in Chapter 3. As the authors pointed out, the senior staff of these units 'represent a large proportion of the leadership of professional educational technologists in the United Kingdom' (CET, 1979, 5). They suggested that in the coming years these members of staff and the facilities for which they are responsible could make a major contribution to the higher education system, by reduction of costs 'provided there is adequate institutional commitment to achieving this aim'. The last phrase way is, of course, an acknowledgement of the difficulties, discussed in Chapter 3, caused by the teacher-centred traditions in further and higher education, and the psychological barriers to change mentioned above. In this chapter, there will be an attempt to consider in rather more detail the likely nature of the contributions that can be predicted and the long-term effects they could have; throughout, the barriers to change will be kept firmly in mind, since they will be kept in place for as long as possible in many institutions.

There seem to be four areas of contribution (not discussed in the pamphlet mentioned above) which can be predicted with some certainty for video. These are *communication* of information on campus and between campuses; *interpretation* of the institution's role to the outside world and perhaps vice versa; *expansion* of the institution's influence in the world outside, both by direct sales of materials and by the development of co-operative activities on a wide range of fronts; finally and most notably, although at first by stealth rather than by more direct means, there seems likely a *transformation* of aspects of teaching, examining and research. In each of these areas, video will itself contribute to the processes of change, and the educational television units discussed in Chapter 3 will, if they survive introverted and reactionary assaults in the early 1980s, have a major role to play. Each of these areas will be discussed in turn, below, and the chapter will conclude with a summary of the possible effects on the position of colleges and universities in the communities they serve.

Communication

Each year, the British Library Bibliographic Services Division publishes a British Education Index, aiming to list and analyse the subject content of all articles of 'permanent educational interest' which have appeared in the English-language periodicals published or distributed in the British Isles. Commenting on his search of that index for 1977-9, the author of 'National Education and the Microelectronics Revolution' noted that 'virtually nothing of any real interest on the subject of microelectronics, microcomputers and microprocessors in education has appeared in serious journals devoted to research and analysis in education in the past three years' (Maddison, 1980, 9). The writer criticised this 'apparent insouciance' as a major long-term problem for education and training, all the more remarkable when one considered the tremendous implications of the subject. Certainly it is interesting that nothing could be found on this subject in any major publication dealing with educational thought and practice. Yet the fact of that silence points to several significant features of microelectronics and tertiary education that are quite distinct. First, the most immediate results of the new technology to be found in this area will probably be in the library; secondly, libraries are singularly ill-prepared, for all the reforms that have been carried out in their own data storage and retrieval systems, to cope with what they themselves sometimes call 'non-book' materials; thirdly, bibliographic resources are only as useful as the ingenuity of those who create them permits. Once again one can quote the old computing tag GIGO ('garbage in, garbage out'), or at least NINO ('nothing in, nothing out').

Libraries in tertiary education have for long offered their users access to far more resources than was true even a decade ago. National networks permit swift access to and transmission of printed material from great distances. This process will extend further in years to come, but the combined influences of the many converging technological developments in video and computing will be to affect libraries and therefore the educational institutions they serve, in a much more radical way. The digitalisation and improved microcircuitry of television systems will encourage not only improved reliability, greater sturdiness and lower costs, but also greater utilisation of video itself to record information (i.e. 'storage') in audio-visual form and swifter and more varied access to it (i.e. 'retrieval'). The real obstacle to such developments is no longer cost but imagination and, most urgently, improved means of indexing. Even if it is strictly true that no article, nor its abstract, in any of the journals listed over the three years 1977-9 by the British Education Index, referred directly to microelectronics in education, it is inconceivable that there was none which could not have been applied in some way to that topic. In the area of video the fact that material with multiple value may not be indexed as such a rich resource has long been a notable problem. Working in Malta 15 years ago as an educational television producer I remember saving from the bonfire film stock produced by government information film units (it had been declared obsolete) and utilising certain sequences in quite different contexts and for quite different purposes than the title of the production (or its synopsis) would have suggested. Catalogues of films or of video material currently and inadequately describe in words what would be inherently difficult (but by no means unimaginable) to enter and index in computerised form under a great range of headings. Browsing through audio-visual material is now also a possibility, as movement forward and back at several times real speed becomes possible, without losing sight of the image.

Telematics will have its own impact on higher education, in various ways. The value of cable systems to some institutions of tertiary education is already considerable, simply as communication channels. As the cable network spreads across Britain the current utilisation of coaxial cable on a single campus to carry, say, ongoing mainframe computer status information to outstations, or campus news and notices, will rapidly expand. The arrival in a few years time of fibre-optic cable technology will give a great boost to these developments and permit libraries, computing services and educational television units to share in exercises to promote the communication of information in a far wider sense than is understood by the phrase at present. To take one pefectly imaginable scenario, fibre-optic cable links on campus or between campuses would make the television conference — currently only in regular use by multinational corporations and the like — a frequently used method of bringing participants together to discuss, demonstrate and inform without having to interrupt their normal routine or pay the costs implied by travelling and/or staying at a remote conference centre. Electronic meetings of this sort in Britain involve small groups of delegates at two or three sites, in touch with each other by British Telecom landlines, sending and receiving live monochrome sound and vision relay of conversations or close-ups of documents (or other small items) for a number of rented hours. The system appears expensive at present but the experience offers a remarkably efficient means of communication that could readily be applied to academic needs. In the United States, where physical distance is a greater problem than in most European countries, the system has proved very useful for organisations with frequent urgent managerial or engineering problems to resolve: Ford and Boeing both use electronic meeting systems regularly. Holiday Inn is already developing both national and international networks as an aid to their existing conventional conference facilities (Walters, 1981). Imaginative application of this commercial resource to academic purposes could involve appropriate use of library, computing and video materials at occasional or even regular meetings of research workers, whether teachers, students or both.

Interpretation

It is ironic that those same educational television units described in Chapter 3 as tending to be objects of suspicion to those with power in tertiary education also tend to be involved more regularly than any other area of the institution in the interpretation of its role to the outside world. If, for example, a college with an educational television unit decides to hold an Open Day, the unit will be overwhelmed (traditionally at short notice) with demands to create, edit, display, design or offer live video resources. This is not just a matter of prestige, of ensuring that the public realises what an up-to-date go-ahead college they are fortunate to be visiting. It is also discovered that to explain and interpret the work of a department is a complicated matter to encapsulate in typescript, that it is unattractive to do so, and that it would be tedious for staff to have to offer guided tours many times on Open Day. Video, in fact, as is often claimed by its practitioners, is a resource capable of interpreting complex ideas in an attractive, lucid form; nowadays video recorders do not get tired in the way they once did, and as humans still do, so that they do not object to multiple repetitions. Prestige is more of a factor when visitors (perhaps from overseas) are coming to the institution to admire and learn from its work: the library and the educational television unit are normal stops on tours without a clear research purpose, as also for visiting dignitaries.

Such units, then, are well used to the difficult role of interpreting aspects of the life of their parent university, polytechnic or college to the world outside. This is a role bound to increase in years to come. The need to market educational courses or training opportunities, already well-known in the United States, will increase. The demographic unevenness and the economic uncertainties of the late twentieth century mean that post-compulsory education will no longer imply for colleges and their peers quietly coping with the selection, teaching and certification of a steadily growing cohort of young adults. There will be even greater needs to recruit specific types of students to ensure continued funding of particular academic activities: such needs will require urgent, accurate and professionally prepared marketing, however uncongenial that idea may at present appear, in appropriate style. The units will be one of the only experienced resources such institutions can call on internally to create suitable material at short notice and at reasonable costs. For many years, most British universities have circulated schools with recruitment films, thinly disguised as information: in 1981 the first 'videoprospectus' was created and disseminated by Leeds

University. Instead of sending and retrieving up to ten bulky 16mm prints at a time, several hundred videocassettes were distributed free of charge to schools on the existing lending list, for optional retention or return. The exercise proved cheaper than the conventional loan system, and was certainly easier; the same may be said of the production costs of the film (made by the University Audio-Visual Service) compared with commissioning from an external production company, lacking the unit's 15 years of campus experience. As telematics continue to have their radical effect on many aspects of society elsewhere, the expectation that information will be prepared with new modes of reception and retrieval in mind will grow, so that the use of video for these sorts of purposes will increase. It is by no means inconceivable that within a few years, presentation of a college's appeal fund or of a research team's case for a grant will be supported by video material. Finally, under the heading of interpretation, European tertiary education institutions will have to get used to the idea, familiar in the United States, that local television news is about to become a much more vigorous activity, and that they themselves are likely to be invited to supply video material to one or more cable channels in the region. These two developments are bound to involve a measure of explanation of the work of the institution: the fortunate will be able to use their existing educational television unit; the less fortunate will have to use a neighbouring unit or set up one of their own from scratch.

Expansion

Education is already recognised by all accountants and by many alert businessmen as something few educators would immediately acknowledge it to be: a highly saleable commodity. Educational video materials, in the form of packages for individual study or to stimulate and guide group training activities, can already command considerable sales if carefully prepared and the distributors of videocassettes are already moving energetically into the field of defining markets, identifying potential creators and commissioning projects for sales. Some of these have already been spectacularly successful. Guild Sound & Vision Ltd, the largest British publisher of film and video materials, in 1981 began distributing 'Basic — An Introduction to Computer Programming', a course designed for individual or group study to introduce the user to the computer language in standard use for microcomputer programming, and to learn to write one's own programs in that language. The course was devised by a senior member of staff at Sheffield University's Computer Services Department and produced by the Senior Television Producer at the university: the video material was actually recorded at another university in the North of England, earning the unit there some useful revenue. Since completion, sales have been excellent, not only to universities but to a number of commercial and industrial users in the United States.

Such a venture is one example of the expansion of the role of individual teachers, of teaching departments and of educational television units, that can be predicted from now on. In the United States such activities have been commonplace for many years, partly because tertiary education has traditionally relied on external revenue and donations to a far greater extent than in Europe, partly because of the enormous market for video materials that has opened up there in the past decade (Lloyd-Kolkin, 1981). As the processes described in this book continue, that market will grow, and colleges, polytechnics and universities that can take advantage of it will be better placed to survive the cold winds blowing over public education in the 1980s than those that cannot. Distribution of video material will be a particularly attractive means of earning revenue, but of course it will be only one facet of a growing market of very considerable economic importance. Britain, like many other European countries, has to make the difficult transition from a major manufacturing country to a society relying much less heavily for its export earnings on traditional industrial goods and markets: 'invisibles' such as banking, tourism, consultancy, as well as education and training, will have to expand considerably to compensate. In the winter of 1981-2, one of Britain's largest building contractors landed a £160 million contract from a state government in West Africa. A crucial factor in winning the deal to build a huge college of technology and institute of mining, was a £3.1 million sub-contract with the British Council (Britain's government agency to promote British education and culture) and the Polytechnic of Central London, to supply a range of courses to enable the new colleges to be staffed by Nigerian teachers. The Council, having taken a 15 per cent management fee, purchased United Kingdom university courses worth £1.25 million, while the Polytechnic supplied its own technician training courses (£1.2 million) and appropriate fellowships in the United States for Nigerian academic staff (£0.5 million). The academic in charge of the Polytechnic's 'International Services' had three academic colleagues and three administrative assistants. Handling business already worth over £500,000 yearly (3 per cent of the Polytechnic's annual budget), the director saw the unit's work expanding, as developing countries continued to build technical training institutions and to require English language training and courses in English (Brown, 1982). Two aspects of this form of expansion are particularly relevant to video in tertiary education. First, the deal described depends for its success on a measure of flexibility in institutional and individual attitudes, a willingness to co-operate with external agencies and to risk effort in the expectation that the results will eventually be worthwhile. The PCL International Services Unit was set up in 1974 and has doubtless had difficulties in the past: it depends for its success, as does the expansion of the work of educational television units, on the identification of academics willing and able to co-operate with the outside world, and on administrative structures with sufficient authority and will to carry through complex contracts, first to the point of signature, then to completion on time and to standard. The second point is that video is a particularly suitable medium in which to prepare large portions of technical training materials for export. While there may be a chance that comprehension of written English by an overseas teacher may not be complete, video sequences designed to demonstrate a technical process or the operation and testing of a device, or the use of an instrument for student experiments can hardly be misunderstood.

Transformation

As has already been stressed at various points, the transformation of teaching and study methods in tertiary education has often been predicted or preached, to little noticeable effect. Traditional methods are time-honoured partly because they manifestly work, and partly because their operation is well understood, offers a great deal of power and authority to the teacher, and relative freedom for him or her to cope with the demands of the role. By contrast, to utilise video implies discussion of content and methods with others and by definition it involves recording material that is potentially available for groups other than one's own students (including groups of fellow teachers) to inspect. The Council for Educational Technology showed its awareness of the barriers to change by emphasising in the document already mentioned that reduction of costs by application of new methods even to existing courses could only be achieved if there is 'a far greater level of institutional commitment to the achievement of this end than has so far been seen' (CET, 1979, 9). As they put it, there has been little incentive to introduce changes of teaching method, while the power of a department has been measured by size of budget and number of staff as well as by academic standing, and while career advancement has depended principally on research achievement measured by publications. Yet the pace and pressure of technological change seems likely to provide a catalyst. Indeed, if an institution's resistance to the transformation of its teaching-learning methods is determined, the likely result will be the relative failure of that institution to expand sales of its courses, interpret clearly to the world its services and, in some circumstances, even to communicate information effectively. It will not, in fact, be as able to compete with its peers for diminishing or at least changing social demands in terms of type of student and type of research project.

This danger was foreseen by the Department of Education and Science in Britain, often criticised for its lack of forward planning, when in 1978 it published a discussion document entitled *Higher Education into the 1990s*. The document described five possible models for higher education in Britain, as demographic and other forces disturbed the traditional reliance on the 18+ cohort to supply highly qualified students. The document, and many comments on it, leaned towards adoption of Model E, the opening up of access to higher education, together with the creation of a much increased range of study materials designed to satisfy the needs of a widely varied range of students. Although the British higher education establishments spurned the suggestion, market and technical forces are likely to impose at least aspects of Model E upon British and indeed other higher education systems in the not-too-distant future. The topic is one of those discussed in the last part of this book.

One of the obstacles that has impeded genuine change in further and higher education has been the poor quality of research into educational technology and higher education. In April 1978, the British Society for Research into Higher Education published the fourth edition of its *Research into Teaching Methods in Higher Education*, the work of three distinguished editors. On the subject of television, to which some four pages of text in one hundred were devoted, the authors cited around 45 sources in support of their judgement that 'television is not a substitute for other methods but a supplement to them' (Beard, Bligh and Harding, 1978, 49). That has a definitive ring to it, unlike many educational research findings. Yet closer study reveals that it was derived from contradictory sources predominantly published in the 1960s (nearly 70 per cent of those cited), with the median year of publication being 1968, and that some of the research mentioned was so trivial (for example that 'because visuals hold attention while the acquisition of information is consolidated by words, visual and auditory material should be closely integrated') as to be not worth quoting. Publishing definitive judgements based on outdated and misdirected research may not pose a problem for the proper understanding of some subjects. In this case there have been crucial technical developments since the mid-1970s. Indeed our greater understanding of student needs and approaches to learning, which is highly relevant, is discussed at length and with much sympathy and wisdom elsewhere in their text. A reappraisal of such a definite statement, relegating television to the role of supplementing other methods, was already overdue in 1978 and common sense alone should prevent its expression in 1983.

The alternative suggestion, that television is a substitute for other methods, a sort of ersatz medium, threatening displacement of well-tried teaching methods and perhaps even of staff, has often been made by those who are suspicious of video for whatever reason, as a straw man to be knocked down as swiftly as possible. I am as ready as the next person to knock down straw men, but it is interesting that one of the most oft-quoted research findings − that the television lecture is not more effective than live lecturing − is always accepted as supporting the continuance of live lecturing. A moment's consideration of the true costs involved in both exercises would suggest to an objective mind that the finding is double-edged: if both methods are equally effective, cost becomes a major consideration. Since this book is not intended to improve teaching methods *per se*, this point is made not to encourage the recording and dissemination of lectures, but rather to underline once again the psychological obstacles impeding the introduction of new study materials and methods into tertiary education. In reality, television has typically been utilised neither as substitute nor as supplement to traditional teaching, but in conjunction with it (a significant difference) or as part of a transformation of it. A good example of co-operation between educational television unit, academic staff and commercial company leading to the development of a new form of teaching is reported by Aikman (1982). After several years of research, a British company is now marketing a device that combines for medical, paramedical and biological students, and indeed engineers, the benefits of video (an individually perfect view of the event with accurate commentary) with the benefit of a permanent record of an experiment's progress. The instrument encodes two channels of physiological data directly through the second audio track of a video recorder on to videotape. When the tape is played back, the experimental data is displayed on the appropriate oscillograph or other device, in perfect synchrony with the visual record and the original audio or an edited sound-track. The advantages in reduced numbers of animal experiments, the 'capture' of rare clinical events or the creation of single examples of demonstrations that are difficult, dangerous or time-consuming to set up are obvious. So too are the possibilities for shrewd academic staff in terms of the making of material that can be marketed in conjunction with the hardware manufacturer.

The latter point may turn out to be of crucial importance as a lubricant to the process of change, since, as Brew has shown, the real obstacles to change in tertiary education are the perceptions that teachers have of innovations, rather than institutional barriers to change, actual experience, and so forth (Brew, 1982). Co-operation between educational television units and academics can create conditions in which valuable progress can be made. To quote one example, a lecturer in Earth Sciences who had devised a way of demonstrating the process of geological deformation by use of a microscope view of the crushing of such homely materials as talcum powder, consulted his television unit concerning video recording of these events. By borrowing the unit's professional electronic news-gathering recorder, the lecturer was able to record long sequences of (incidentally very beautiful) simulations that could then be edited into appropriate study materials in the University Television Centre. At another university in Northern England, computer graphics techniques have been used to decipher twelfth-century Ethiopian manuscripts (since the computer has greater patience and skill than the human eye in comparing and recognising handwritten characters) and in the analysis of bone structures and deformities for medical and surgical purposes (Lewell, 1981, 754). Co-operation between computer scientist, video unit and academic can already create novel material for study via the application of modern technology to research. This sort of teamwork may well lead to the construction of new bridges by which to enter citadels that have so long withstood change.

In 1976 I wrote in a journal called *University Vision* that the relationship between the academic and the producer was the crucial difficulty facing the latter of engaging co-operation from those academics who regarded the producer as 'a sort of amanuensis to the blind sage, who should be left free to express his own views in an unfamiliar medium' (Moss, 1976, 37). It is true that the arrogance of certain members of that noble profession, the academic, towards their colleagues in academic services (an appropriate label) has to be experienced to be believed. It has been aptly described in the dictum of Sir Peter Venables: 'I am pure; you are applied; he is technological'. Since 1976 many more examples than hitherto have been seen of the kind of co-operation which will be necessary for the transformation of aspects of the university experience. Although the course team approach pioneered by the Open University towards the combined creation by academics, educational technologists and production staff has been seen hardly at all in conventional universities and colleges as yet, there has been evidence of Open University materials being introduced into conventional institutions not only by Open University tutors but by others (G.D. Moss, 1979). We are still an enormous distance away, in psychological terms, from academic acceptance of some novel possi-bilities. For example, students may eventually be able to carry out many of the library study elements of their work from home; the lecture aspect of courses could and should be drastically reduced in the university of the future. Such developments would not, of course, reduce the need for small-group or individual tuition, 'the essential core of higher education where the student is able to test his newly gained ideas against a highly trained mind. Quite the reverse is the case.' (CET, 1979, 14). That is the irony. Resistance to change in the traditional approaches, although protecting authoritarian positions, in fact leaves both students and teachers locked into the least rewarding relationships imaginable for study in higher education. To reduce the amount of lecturing encourages more satisfactory and valuable con-tacts, transferring parts of the essential teaching load to other formats.

Video also has a key role to play in the whole area of examination, especially of students whose professional certification involves practi-cal experience. The assessment of physicians' clinical skills used tradi-tionally to be carried out by presenting them with a number of patients on whom diagnosis had to be carried out, followed by a range of ques-tions from examiners on what the student had observed or elicited from the patient, and clinical judgements on the observations. Such a proce-dure was obviously prone to error. A number of studies long ago repor-ted promising results from making videotape recordings of patient interviews, ensuring standardised evidence was presented to examina-tion students, on which standard questions could be asked and respon-ses then coded for accurate assessment. The application of this tech-nique for the examination of students of psychiatry has been shown to be advantageous, given, for example, the unreliability of patient be-haviour in an interview situation (Muslin, Thumblad, Templeton *et al.*, 1974). In 1979, videotaped case histories were introduced as an option ('short case') technique in the final MB (Psychiatry) examination by London teaching hospitals. A preliminary investigation (Jolly, 1981) studied possible disadvantages of the procedure. These centred on the points that students were not eliciting information themselves (although some found the edited material, obviously condensed to concentrate on significant factors, easier to absorb) and that the fact of material having been edited was somewhat distracting in itself. On the other hand, there was a broad measure of agreement that the procedure was worth development, as a useful assessment procedure. It was noted that it was possible, as one examiner put it, to give 'predictable demonstrations of psychopathology without embarrassment to the patient, student or examiner, or to the ward where the examinations were held'. Extension of these techniques to other areas of both training and examination would be perfectly possible. Social workers, teachers, and indeed members of almost every profession can share in the advantages of the application. The approach is particularly appropriate for in-service training centred on the introduction of new techniques, changes in the law and so forth. Ethical problems afforded by the retention of 'sensitive' interviews may be met by the creation of simulated material and/or by measures to disguise participants or to destroy material after use in a single training course or examination.

There are therefore powerful forces drawing tertiary education institutions towards transformation of some of their methods of teaching and examining. Research itself, including methods of storing, publishing and retrieving information, can be expected to alter, even if one is for the present sceptical about the possibilities of creating an electronic academic journal (Peters, 1981). More immediate changes are likely to occur in tertiary education because of the social effects implied by the advance of video discussed in Chapter 5:

> the developing centrality of the home base for learning is likely in the 80s to be set in a very different institutional context. Paradoxically, perhaps, the perceived strengths of independent learning for individuals do not seem easily to extend to the present or future shape of educational institutions. A spirit of institutional autonomy has been a significant and arguably damaging feature of United Kingdom post-compulsory education to date . . . It exists not only in an internecine fashion within and between sectors of education, but also globally in the still too frequently hostile stance of education over against para-educational interests. (Richardson, 1980, 20)

For a host of reasons already outlined at various points, both these traditional ivory tower stances (towards other towers, and towards the rest of the community, especially those parts with an interest in the tower's business) are likely to shift in the latter part of the twentieth century. Heavy government funding in Britain and elsewhere for the work of quasi-educational bodies such as the Manpower Services Commission in Britain, for example, is bound to attract the attention of the university sector. Some will have noted remarks made by government spokesmen in 1982 that some of the money to be released for the Open Tech comes from funds withdrawn from higher education. Institutions of tertiary education capable to adapting part of their activities to creating and supplying materials for the Open Tech can regain some of the funds being lost through cuts elsewhere. Those that will not or cannot adapt will lose ground to their competitors. Similar opportunities obtain elsewhere, and will be bound to increase as the home base for video-centred study and entertainment becomes even more significant to the citizens of the future. In sum, the post-compulsory education sector can choose to ignore the opportunities offered by video to alter patterns of study. If so, decline seems inevitable. The alternative strategy will involve a co-operative response to the challenge to devise new schemes designed to open up scholarship to wider, more dispersed and very different students than have been experienced before.

Part Three

VIDEO AND NEW PATTERNS OF STUDY

8 VIDEO IN DISTANCE LEARNING

Although by definition television ('vision over a distance') has long been involved in distance learning, the rich colours of video's roles in new patterns of distance learning have yet to be imagined, let alone brought into play. Most attempts to do so have to date involved simple adaptation of existing schemes of study or relegation of the video element to a minor contribution. The future is likely to offer particularly intriguing prospects for new usages. In dicussing routes over this new territory, it will be important to refer at length to the work of the Open University, Britain's most ambitious distance learning institution, and its predicted future, which includes an increasingly important video element for a wide spectrum of purposes. The experience of the Open University will be very valuable to those trying to devise new patterns of study in the next decade. More conventional projects, like the North American development of video courses, are also booming and their successes and the reasons for them are worthy of note. An extraordinarily varied and promising prospect seems to beckon those with the skill to design and market distance-learning packages to support the much expanded purposes of educational institutions in the latter part of the twentieth century.

Most experiences of distance learning have so far been with adults, since compulsory full-time education is now the norm for children at primary level, and for most societies at secondary level, too. Except for those children who are separated from their schools by physical barriers or the remoteness of their home, distance learning has been an adult experience. This may change in future, as new patterns of study are developed, and certainly our understanding of distance learning for adults will be applicable to children's use of such courses also. For it seems clear that the basic principles for successful human learning apply both to children and adults: strong motivation and plenty of activity. Adults of low intelligence, probably because of their unsatisfactory school (and life) experiences, tend to deteriorate in learning capacity as they grow older; highly intelligent adults are less likely to lose their intellectual ability as they age. An excellent 1977 handbook for teachers of adults summarises the main features of adult learning as follows:

Adults learn best when they do not have to rely on memorising, but can learn through activity at their own pace with material that seems relevant to their daily lives and uses their own experience. Finding 'right' answers at the first attempt seems important. Generous practice will reinforce new skills. Adults who have been out of touch with learning can often improve their educational performance dramatically if they are helped by learning to learn. (Rogers, 1977, 59)

Jennifer Rogers' book stresses, with many examples from student interviews, the problems faced by adult students who are required to rely heavily on short-term memory, and to learn passively at a pace set by some external force, a learning experience typified by the lecture. At the same time, one of the problems associated with distance learning is the lack of social and emotional support provided by the conventional teacher-and-class situation. Adult learners tend to lack confidence and to lose heart easily; distance learning can be a lonely experience. A distinguished writer on educational method, Professor Donald Bligh, has warned that innovations in study methodology will fail if they demote the importance for adult learners of 'socio-emotional support' provided by the human interaction of small-group study (Bligh, 1977).

There is of course no need for the use of multi-media learning resources to imply that at all. The Open University has demonstrated with considerable success that it is possible to combine a correspondence-based approach to study with occasional face-to-face tuition (and student groups), as well as television and radio broadcasts, and a week-long residential summer school. The use of a multi-media teaching approach is the best-known characteristic of the Open University. Other factors are just as significant for the adult distance learner. The degrees awarded are general, not specific to a particular discipline; they are gained after successful completion of a number of courses, for each of which a full credit or half-credit is earned, at a rate governed by the student's own circumstances. The university has an increasingly skilled support system (full-time professional staff in the region of a student's home, part-time tutors and counsellors, and a range of documentary and other forms of advice and help); from the first, the Institute of Educational Technology has undertaken a primary duty to monitor, research and improve the institution's teaching methods and support services. A student taking an Open University course receives about every four to six weeks packs of study materials and an assignment, to be returned for assessment by computer or by a local part-time tutor. In addition, the student is aided by radio and television broadcasts designed and produced by the team of academics and producers responsible for the correspondence materials and assignments. Every year, any student taking a full-credit course is required to attend a week-long 'summer school' at one of Britain's conventional universities: these are, in my own experience, intensely exciting events, as distance learners come together in large numbers to enjoy 'for one week only', the flavour of residential undergraduate life. These occasions, as well as the several regional tutorials a student attends each year, are vivid evidence for most participants in the Open University venture of the success of the institution in coping with the disparate needs of thousands of adult distance learners, and above all providing that human support to which Professor Bligh referred, while using imaginatively created materials for study, in a wide range of media.

The core of the Open University course consists of the correspondence texts. The best of these, whether from the Open University or from other sources, combine certain common features. They state and refer systematically to planned objectives; they are presented in a professionally designed form in a skilled manner intended to attract and retain interest by use of illustrations, diagrams and a well-judged style. Above all, they involve the student actively. A typical correspondence text will be broken up by a line or mark at various points, inviting the student to stop, carry out a minor experiment or read two or three relevant passages, then reach a conclusion on a question that has been raised, before returning to the text, where the issue is discussed. The tone throughout the most effective Open University course units is deceptively off-hand and cheerful, suggesting an enthusiasm for discovery and discussion without underlining the structure of a carefully planned argument in which the student has participated. It is in fact a Socratic approach appropriate both for unqualified students gaining open access to higher education, and to overcome the disadvantages of distance learning. The Open University's part-time tutors are encouraged to develop a similar tone in their written comments on student work, which are intended to guide students not only towards a more successful judgement on a set question, but also on how to organise an essay better, how to use an index, how to get the best out of the multi-media materials.

More subtly than this the tutor needs to write comments which deliberately acknowledge that he has absorbed what the student was trying to achieve. For instance, 'I see that you have thoroughly read

X's book and I agree with your comments on his general theories. However, when you come to Z, I think you should re-read his section on Y where you may come to the conclusion that . . . My own feeling is that, although . . .' A tone like this, which perhaps seems at first contrivedly tentative, nevertheless allows the student to retain his self-esteem, flatters him by showing him that his tutor has taken him seriously and yet still allows him space to reconsider his original judgement. (Rogers, 1977, 185)

As has been discussed in Chapter 1, learning seems, as Socrates himself demonstrated, to be based on conversations: Gordon Pask and his associates have in fact developed a comprehensive approach to cognitive psychology, a 'theory of conversations, individuals and knowables', that rests upon consideration of the results of experiments to observe human methods of classifying (and learning from) unfamiliar information (Daniel, 1975, 88). Such 'conversations' may take place within a student's own mind, where he or she is considering and extending understanding from 'knowables' in, say, a distance learning text. To that extent all learning can be described as interactive. The Vice-President of one of Canada's own open distance learning institutions, Athabasca University, formerly at Quebec's celebrated Télé-Université, has discussed in a valuable paper the ways in which interaction (student contact with other people) and independence can best be blended in distance education. This article will be discussed in more detail below (Daniel and Marquis, 1977).

When discussing the need for in-service training in Chapter 6, reference was made to an ingenious self-instructional guide to the writing of self-instructional materials, produced by the Open University Centre for International Co-operation and Services (Rowntree and Connors, 1979). This offers both practical guidance and guided practice for teachers embarking on the creation of self-instructional materials either for distance learning or on-campus students. In introducing the principles lying behind the guide, produced by a team from the Open University's Institute of Educational Technology, one of the co-editors identifies 'evaluation and improvement' as the driving force for the design of self-instructional materials (Connors, 1979, 82). The strength of that drive has been notable in the first decade of the work of the Open University, which has constantly to engage, by means of numerous feedback channels, in what has been called 'the somewhat agonising process of self-improvement' (McIntosh, 1976, 20). This process has included not only the steady accumulation of knowledge about general principles of design for effective multi-media distance learning materials, but specific exercises in what has been called 'formative evaluation'. This topic was the subject of heated discussion at the 1976 international conference on Research and Evaluation in educational television and radio, organised by the Open University, in association with UNESCO and other bodies (Bates and Robinson, 1977). The phrase is used to cover the process of investigating by pre-testing (and application of previous experience) the value of a particular technique or piece of teaching, and then making changes to the material, or even to policy on the use of that type of material for a particular purpose, prior to distribution. The process has frequently been applied in the production of correspondence courses and occasionally for educational television programmes. It is, of course, also used in the area of advertising. A seminar organised by the Council for Educational Technology in 1978 discussed three examples of pre-testing television material, a BBC series for mentally handicapped children ('Let's Go'), an ITV pre-school series (Granada's 'Daisy, Daisy') and the use of pre-testing in preparing commercials for television. If any common conclusion emerged from the seminar, it was that formative evaluation could reveal insights into education television material valuable both to producer and teacher, but that these would only be taken into account if the evaluation had been planned as an integral part of the creative production process.

One of the most intriguing aspects of the Open University venture has been the development of the course team approach to creativity, to which reference has been made several times already. Whereas formative evaluation is difficult for a broadcasting organisation (or, for that matter, conventional educational institution) to accommodate, the administration of course team control of production implies that formative evaluation is perfectly possible in that context. Teamwork between professionals with different training and responsibilities relies on mutual respect and a carefully planned schedule: formative evaluation can be built into such a schedule if it is accepted as an essential contribution to effective design from the outset of a team's co-operation. Of course its inclusion does not guarantee smooth agreement between the team at all times; it does offer the prospect of evidence to support or overthrow views otherwise based on individual experiences that are likely to conflict. Of course such evaluation exercises cost money (the Children's Television Workshop spent 46 million dollars developing the formula for 'Sesame Street') and/or time; both may be in short supply. Distance learning schemes, however, will be most effective when they have a relatively long production run and when they attract a relatively large number of clients. Both criteria are more likely to be met with adequate pre-testing; without it a distance learning package may never travel anywhere.

Daniel and Marquis define as modes of *interaction* in a distance learning scheme contact with counsellors, or tutors, interactive tele-communication, discussion groups and residential gatherings. The term *independence* is used by them to cover study of written material, watching or listening to television or radio materials, writing, working alone at a computer terminal, home experiments, and project or survey works (Daniel and Marquis, 1977, 30). The message of this book suggests that, as Daniel and Marquis would probably readily acknow-ledge, these groupings will in future be by no means as hard and fast in their divisions as they are at present. In any case, the educational approach of Pask and others, regarding learning as participation in a conversation, itself implies that skilful design of materials for independ-ent learning will involve interactivity. Specifically, it is already possible to utilise video receivers in an interactive manner, addressing major computers at a distance or using one's own computer, either on its own or in combination with other devices such as video recorders. Once video materials are available (initially through a regional office, in future direct to the student) in the student's home, they can be de-signed not as broadcast programmes but as self-instructional materials akin to the textual units that form the core of correspondence courses. Indeed they can converge with them (as has been imagined or seen in other contexts). A piece of video could invite student self-testing or become central to assessed assignment work or examination questions, as a course team takes account of changing needs and opportunities. The underlying dynamic for such changes is the idea of the course team itself, enforcing definition of objectives and discussion of course con-tent and methods of presentation among a group of teachers and other professionals.

Another form of convergence that can already be seen, because of research evidence on adult learning from broadcast television, is between the work of broadcasters and that of educational television units. Evaluation work has demonstrated that Open University students tend to have two types of problems with Open University television broadcasting. These relate either to the utilisation of the programme's content ('what was it trying to tell me?') or to the viewing of general output material normally being a passive, relaxed experience, so that it is difficult for some students to make the shift of attitude required to take full advantage of the broadcast. So concerned has the Institute of Educational Technology become about this that it has produced a package of materials entitled 'Learning from Television', consisting of a videocassette to illustrate the range of Open University broadcasts and associated written papers and exercises. The advice given to students may be summarised as encouraging the development of an active rather than passive approach to viewing, recognising that some broadcasts require a high level of activity (application of a theory to a particular set of circumstances), while others explain an argument, offer a specific experience or provide a case to be studied (Durbridge, 1981). As has already been suggested, the idea of educational television as typically broadcast is unlikely to survive much longer. As video usage increases, the proportion of students requiring specific help with the problem of how most effectively to use video designed for educational use is likely to fall. There are two reasons for this. First, those who produce educational video for individual study will create material unlike programmes to be broadcast, to take account of the student's new ability to control the pace (and even order) of viewing. Secondly, students who will increasingly gain greater control of the viewing experience will be less likely to be passive viewers. Convergence will encourage course teams to design video material in a style (including 'student-stoppers') much more like the written units and content will include at the outset a clear statement of objectives for the video item, just as in texts.

Even before the video revolution has got under way, new patterns of multi-media study had been devised. In Canada, TV Ontario introduced a 'new concept in adult learning' in 1980. Television broadcasts combine with a computer-managed learning system and specially prepared texts to give viewers the opportunity to embark upon self-directed projects, extending over several weeks. The broadcasts cover 'a well-defined body of knowledge' (e.g. 'Health and the Environment') and are either specially produced or purchased from elsewhere. The computerised contribution (in process of adaptation from IBM 360/370 to microcomputer operation) is to react to student responses to a set of multiple-choice questions with an individualised letter. 90 per cent of the students enjoy receiving these, finding them helpful, stimulating and relevant; the majority are satisfied with the language and writing style of the letters (Waniewicz, 1981). It is noteworthy that the experience gained in this ingenious, if at present expensive, venture has underlined once again the necessity for close co-operation between academic subject specialists, educational technologists and experts in production of both television and computer programmes. The Russell Report on Adult Education called in 1973 for 'analogues to the Open University at a lower level. By this term we mean multi-media systems combining teaching at a distance with face-to-face tuition, some relatively permanent, others transitory or perhaps ephemeral', and for an 'organisational framework' within which 'learning systems could be established involving different media and agencies' (Department of Education and Science, 1973).

The Open University itself has developed a Centre for Continuing Education, offering distance learning opportunities for some 30,000 non-degree students annually (already about half the total number of degree students). Initial experiments have been expanded sharply in recent years, especially in the area of scientific and technological updating (SATUP). The first of these, a microprocessor course for managers, consisted of a distance learning pack of text and experimental kit, but no video material, nor indeed assignment work (Horlock, 1982, 7). Future developments are certain to involve video material for home-based study. The Open University has been paying particular attention to recent American experience in this area, especially the swift advance of the Association for Media-Based Continuing Education (AMCEE) which has assembled a formidable array of video-centred distance learning courses. Twenty-two universities are now involved, offering video recordings of lecture courses in engineering, economics and management. Such materials can be studied at home or at work, at low cost to employer or individual, and, of course, are entirely up to date. By 1980, over 35,000 engineers were participating annually in video-based retraining courses at their job site (Stephen, 1982, 4). The AMCEE courses are particularly attractive to the academic institutions participating because they involve little interference with normal teaching (standard lectures are recorded, in a lecture theatre, at the lowest cost). They attract clients and their employers because they involve less expense than conventional retraining courses (no travel or subsistence costs) and less disruption (no ego threat to individual student, studying on his/her own at convenient times). The current AMCEE view is that clients prefer standard lectures recorded on campus to specially made material, a generalisation too broad to sustain. In years to come, as the range of video-based materials extend, there is little doubt that their style will also vary with particular purpose and usage. As AMCEE already notes, whereas a conventional lecture is ephemeral and restricted in audience, even a straight recording of the same lecture can be reconsidered, modified and/or incorporated in other material.

Adaptability was a key feature of the Open Tech concept that was being developed in Britain in 1982. It was clear from the report of the Open Tech Task Group, published in July 1982, that the methods and materials envisaged for this new programme for the training and re-training of technicians are intended to be varied, imaginative and as 'open' in access as possible (Manpower Services Commission, 1982, 7). The attempt to remove barriers to access (on which see below, Chapter 9) is seen as closely linked to providing a wide range of learning opportunities including not only the most recent forms of video-based study and computer-based materials, but also tuition of the tried and tested traditional method. It remains to be seen how successful will be the concept of collaboration between the very small Open Tech Unit and institutions offering Open Tech Projects. The Open University has operated since its inception as an independent institution, providing all materials and arrangements for tuition and examination of its students. By contrast, the Open Tech has been planned as an enabling agency, providing pump-priming funds to support 'a planned and co-ordinated range of commissioned projects . . .[providing] open learning opportunities for specific target groups through the design, production and updating of learning materials'. The essential lubricant for collaboration (and for the submission of project proposals) will, of course, be the funding, but the ideal of 'constructive collaboration' is a bold concept now being tested in a larger arena than the Open University. Indeed, as has been pointed out, the scale of the Open Tech Programme is comparatively so vast that it was bound to be planned as an open-learning system, not a second Open University. For 'a central Open Tech would sink under its own weight, so the only hope for the Open Tech is to stimulate others to do its work for it' (Freeman, 1982, 9). The scale of the exercise also implies that there will have to be heavy reliance on new methods of study: the 1982 Report acknowledged the need to take advantage of computer-assisted and audio-visual study methods, without perhaps fully recognising that the need to store, adapt, replicate, exchange and update learning materials would swiftly become overwhelming if particularly heavy use were not made of these methods.

Video, then, is promised a major role in the new Open Tech production. It is to be hoped that it will also be seen as possessing many useful attributes to play a similarly important part in distance education in the Third World. There can be no doubt about the significance of distance education itself in the development of the social and economic health of Third World countries. Increasingly, the nations of the Southern hemisphere are beginning to accept the arguments of Paolo Freire of Brazil, in seeing education as liberation: education needs to become 'the action and reflection of men upon their world in order to transform it'. To that end, distance education is seen as a key weapon in the struggle to resolve the enormous problem of societies in which the majority of citizens of all ages lack basic education. Whereas the post-colonial tradition, understandably and with worthy intention, concentrated on attempting to provide formal systems of instruction derived from Western models, it is now argued that distance education can and should use a process approach to inspire problem-solving skills among the predominantly agrarian populations of the Third World. Others argue that provision of a basic education for all (literacy, numeracy, health) should be the prime purpose of distance education.

The place of video in distance education programmes for Third World countries is by no means assured. Reference was made in Chapter 2 to the unhappy experience of the 1960s, with ambitious and oversold educational television schemes disappointing many through administrative, technical or pedagogic failures. The enormous expense of television transmission and production equipment and of training (and retaining) the skilled staff needed to man it will remain problems for any nation contemplating investment in a full-scale broadcasting service. To quote two examples from East Africa, a 1978 survey of educational broadcasting in Kenya showed that, although there were some 70,000 television sets in use and transmission could reach about half the population, television had not been used other than as an entertainment/information medium (Coldevin, 1980, 62). In Tanzania in 1978, President Nyerere had steadfastly resisted pressure to introduce television to the mainland at all, although radio was being heavily used for 'mass mobilisation' distance learning campaigns in the areas of health, literacy, nutrition and citizenship (Coldevin, 1979, 72). President Nyerere has published a series of essays on the subject of 'education for self-reliance', in which he criticises the failure of schools to relate to the communities from which their pupils are drawn, and radio has been used to try to leap over what is seen as that barrier (Katz and Wedell, 1978, 130). Professor Coldevin cited some of the problems surrounding just one such radio campaign, 'Food is Life', mounted in 1975. The campaign was adversely affected by its own success: its target number of participants (1.5 million) was exceeded by 30 per cent, so that textbook numbers were inadequate. Many batches of textbooks arrived late; study group leaders were inadequately prepared; the campaign was transmitted during the dry season but naturally referred to skills that could only be implemented later in the year. Worse still, the campaign coincided with two other major educational/political campaigns, a national literacy examination and a general election, all involving most study group leaders and group members (Coldevin, 1979, 74).

Such disappointments do not at all devalue the potential of radio for distance education in the Third World; they merely underline the importance of careful implementation, administration and evaluation, perhaps organised at regional or local level rather than nation-wide. As has already been mentioned, report of a 'failure', however relative, for a novel form of education, at once stimulates a vigorous, conservative reaction from the waiting critics. Frequently, the new baby has been thrown out with the dirty bath-water of experience. In the particular context of distance teaching for the Third World, it is particularly important that every relevant method should be utilised to try to overcome the enormous problems facing such states. A recently published book on the subject describes distance teaching in non-formal contexts such as literacy or rural skills as a 'clockwork mouse' able to nibble through the myriad bonds restraining the 'lion' of formal orthodox educational systems (Young *et al.* 1980). As the costs of video production and replay equipment, as well as software, fall, and as reliability increases, the possibility of using video to assist in Third World educational campaigns should be seriously and imaginatively considered. Just as generals seem doomed always to begin military campaigns with the weapons and methods of the last war, there is a tendency for educational planners to write off last year's failed techniques when planning tomorrow's initiatives. As has been emphasised many times in this book, this has never been a more dangerous practice than at this juncture. The Third World in particular needs to beware that ignoring the challenge and promise of video does not further widen the yawning gap between educational provision in the North and in the South.

A key element in the concept of video as a prime communicative and educative medium, is its potential to bring together distant individuals, offering shared experience. Current technology has hardly begun to explore the possible national and even international collaborative ventures that are at least conceivable as the video revolution continues. Given will and imagination, the lion of education can be freed at last and, with his freedom, individual liberties will be enhanced: video has a role of great importance to play in this movement.

9 VIDEO IN OPEN LEARNING

> For all knowledge and wonder (which is the seed of knowledge) is an impression of pleasure itself. (Francis Bacon, *Advancement of Learning*, 1.1.3)

What is 'open learning'? A UNESCO study has described it as an imprecise phrase, eluding definition, but having great potential 'as an inscription to be carried in procession on a banner, gathering adherents and enthusiasm' (Mackenzie, Postgate and Scupham, 1975). Can one distinguish between the experience of an individual, studying at some distance from the institution responsible for tuition (i.e. distance learning) and the experience of an individual studying alone and unsupervised most of the time (i.e. 'open learning', at least as defined by some)? If that distinction is useful, how can video play a distinctive part in the promotion of the latter experience? In this chapter, once open learning has been defined a little more clearly, the role of video in 'openness' will re-emerge readily enough. As one talks about it, certain psychological aspects of the use of video for study will have to be mentioned and the chapter will close with some thoughts on the future of video in open learning.

On the subject first of the meaning of 'open learning', it will be sufficient for the moment to remark that the relationship with other phrases such as 'distance learning' (or independent/individualised learning) is not a true source of confusion. There is considerable overlap between the phrases and most specific examples of the one may also be cited as examples of the other. If one thinks of open learning systems one is reduced to repeating the rather vague definition offered by Spencer in a recent paper on the subject: 'the word "open" seems to be used where it is wished to emphasise that the system being described is more readily accessible than conventional courses with the same learning objectives' (Spencer, 1980, 19). If one thinks of open learning as an ideal rather than a system, one is back under that banner again, this time with one of the most influential British thinkers on this subject:

> the learning opportunity [should be] available to any person, at any level, at any time, at any place and in any subject. Yes, I mean that you should be able to do Chinese at three o'clock in the morning in

a Welsh mountain village, or learn multiplication tables at 4 p.m. in central Birmingham. (Freeman, 1976)

When Richard Freeman delivered his own characteristically emphatic definition of openness, such an ideal seemed almost unimaginable, a quixotic description of an unattainable objective. Yet so far and so fast has technology already advanced that both the examples he quoted are already feasible, within seven years of his describing them. The problem facing those who plan open learning opportunities is not technical (probably it never was), but educational: it is not providing the delivery opportunity but creating suitable materials and support for them that bedevils open learning. In Chapter 2 of this book there was an enthusiastic welcome for the recent creation in Britain by the independent television companies of a cadre of Community and Continuing Education Officers (CCEOs), whose role would be to devise and develop suitable 'follow-up' opportunities for viewers of certain ITV programmes. I also mentioned Northern Open Learning (NOL), a group of broadcasters, educators, journalists and others endeavouring to create open learning opportunities for audiences of general output broadcasts rather than those defined as educational. The CCEOs were envisaged as providing similar open learning opportunities, but the first period of their activity has been marked by a remarkable caution and hesitation over the co-operation such opportunities imply. That is perhaps not really so surprising. The radical approach to educational broadcasting adopted by Northern Open Learning since its inception almost justifies its portentous title, despite the small membership and (as they themselves readily admit) minor achievements to date of the group. From the first, general output broadcasting was the area of interest, because of its large audiences, and its attractions for all sectors of the population, especially those without formal educational background beyond the statutory age. The group has also several times agreed that its purpose has been to attract or stimulate viewers to follow up interests aroused by broadcasting in their own way, providing a variety of opportunities to do so, rather than to arrange for elaborate systems of traditional adult education courses.

Nevertheless, some form of 'support' is clearly needed to encourage those who do not know how to follow up their interest in a broadcast to do so. The NOL operation aimed to identify a programme or series well in advance of transmission, to alert agencies that might provide support for viewers following up a programme, to persuade the broadcasters to invite viewers to do so and to create a pamphlet detailing local and regional opportunities for free distribution. Although to many broadcasters 'follow up' to a broadcast is synonymous with a publication or publications, this activity is in fact the least important. A publication, even one designed to promote action, is unlikely to do much on its own. Rather, the purpose of NOL has been to encourage viewers of popular television to feel that 'they' (that is, those responsible for television) recognise that viewers may want to know more about an issue or topic, and that those responsible for libraries, museums, art galleries, schools, colleges and even bookshops expect and welcome vague, uninformed interest aroused by viewing to be expressed. Better still, 'they' (whether television or other agencies are meant) may regard the myriad messages of television not as rockets fired into the atmosphere at random, as some television producers sometimes seem to imply, nor as distractions drawing the public away from what they *ought* to be doing, as some educators seem to say, but as a joint responsibility, a co-operative venture. The provision of accessible opportunities for further study by such co-operative actions, with the emphasis on the word 'accessible', provides a sound example of what is meant by 'open learning'.

The follow-up interest engendered in the Yorkshire region by the 'Disraeli' project sponsored by Northern Open Learning was such that 4,000 requests were received for the pamphlet listing open learning opportunities in the area. A high proportion of these came from South Leeds addresses, a predominantly working-class area, demonstrating that a brief 'trailer' at the end of each of four plays, inviting enquiries, could attract substantial responses from individuals not drawn to conventional adult education. By contrast, the ecology workbook prepared in support of 'Botanic Man', a lavish education series watched by millions of viewers nationally in 1978-9, brought only 3,300 enquiries, against predictions of between 30,000 and 100,000. Admittedly, the follow-up trailer (a 30-second voice-over announcement at the end of each of the ten transmissions) had also to sponsor a major coffee-table 'book of the series', a project book for children, and local classes in London (few of which actually took place). This plethora of announcements was probably confusing. Of the 3,300 who did enquire about the ten-unit ecology workbook *The Green Earth*, only 260 actually enrolled to receive it, at a cost – a barrier to many – of £18 (Freeman, 1979, 23). Freeman also suggests that a further barrier may conceivably have been the entertaining style of the television series, implying to the viewer that the experience of viewing 'Botanic Man' could not possibly have anything to do with learning. If so, that would merely

suggest that further trials of linking such materials to popular programmes are desirable, for if this psychological barrier exists it is not a large
one.

The fact of the matter, surprisingly enough, is that very little is
known about the sort of psychological barrier that Freeman postulates.
It does seem rather unlikely that a popularly styled peak-hour educational broadcast ('Botanic Man') should prove to be more of an obstacle to viewers enquiring about follow-up than a popularly styled
peak-hour drama ('Disraeli'). Nevertheless, there is now some definite
evidence concerning the slightly different but related concern that
viewers who habitually watch television to relax may find it harder
to 'use' video material than is expected. This is likely to be more of
a problem for adult learners, especially those making tentative steps
towards study in general as an activity: years of passivity may set
some viewers in a subconscious attitude they find difficult to alter,
whatever their conscious intention. On the other hand, since so much
more information is nowadays presented to the citizen in audio-visual
form, it is at least arguable that open learning opportunities which are
offered in a preponderantly written format may pose even greater
barriers of their own to other groups of adult learners.

At the Open University a series of investigations of student reaction
to and use of television broadcasts led members of the Institute of
Educational Technology to argue in the late 1970s with increasing
emphasis that the video revolution was of considerable significance
for Open University students. It would offer them obvious but vital
educational benefits that would at last assure better returns from the
relatively very expensive television productions that have always
formed part of the Open University study experience (Dallos, 1980).
Mention has already been made of the Open University package of
materials designed to help students develop an awareness of the different demands of the specially prepared television programmes and the
best ways to answer such demands (Durbridge, 1981, 83). As well as
a videocassette describing and exemplifying different types of broadcast, the package contains written papers and exercises aiming to
clarify the ways students are typically expected to respond to broadcasts. Four groups of programmes are distinguished. First, some introduce a theory and invite viewers later to identify examples and classify
them by use of the theory: these are programmes requiring a high level
of activity during a programme. A second group requires students to
carry out the much easier procedure of following and understanding
an argument or process: 'easier' because the process is familiar from

conventional teaching. Much more difficult for students is the third group, in which a specific illustrative experience may be offered, an experience (e.g. a drama or an unfamiliar idea) that is typical of viewing certain types of television documentary. Students sometimes find it difficult to reflect on such a particular experience, placing it in the context of the rest of their course and analysing it by reference to other learning: group discussion can overcome the problem. A final group of programmes, the case study (simply a visual description of naturally occurring events) also poses problems, especially for inexperienced students.

Dr Tony Bates has made a notable summary of the Audio-Visual Media Research Group's tentative findings for the Open University on the unique characteristics of television as a medium (Bates, 1981). It is not as straightforward, perhaps, for the would-be 'open learner' as some, including myself, had predicted. Certainly, the shift from broadcast television to video offers the learner far greater control of his or her learning activity; it offers availability on demand, the ability to repeat a sequence, to stop and start at will and even to hold a single frame for analysis. On the other hand, the enormous richness of the range of modes in which television can present or represent knowledge tells us nothing of itself about how (or indeed 'if') the user processes that knowledge. Television, in other words, is a skilled and gifted *teacher*, able to call on an immensely wide range of resources to present an idea; we understand much less about the *learner*, that is, about how the viewer develops skills to analyse and process that knowledge presented in television format. At the Open University, the Audio-Visual Media Research Group carried out a careful survey of the stated teaching aims of a series of television documentary-style case studies and also studied both the actual content of the programmes and the reaction of the students. The findings offer a warning to all those planning to use video as a major resource in open learning exercises. As mentioned earlier, such case studies are intended to provide descriptions of real-life situations identified by the course team as highly relevant to theoretical material covered by correspondence texts already studied. Students were expected to apply what they had learned, generalising from the particular situation examined, and evaluating the applicability of general principles enunciated in the text to the real-world situation in the television programme. In several cases, these programmes in fact offered the only opportunity in the course for students to practise such skills of application, generalisation and evaluation. Yet for some of the programmes investigated, most students did not see the programmes as relevant or helpful and, for most of the programmes, a large minority of students (about a third) misunderstood the function of the material, expecting it to offer new content or explanation of difficult passages in the correspondence text. Although about one third of students understood the purpose of the programmes, they appeared unable to use them in the way intended. These findings are disturbing for the Open University. In response, there has now been developed the learning package mentioned above, to exemplify typical teaching uses for television and to suggest how to learn most effectively from them. Although the greater learner control offered by video usage should of itself serve to reduce the problems encountered by some students, the unique characteristics of the video medium as distinct from the correspondence text, may continue to pose a barrier to some open learners. After all, as Bates has pointed out, we know little about

> how learning from one medium is integrated with learning from other media, then converted into another medium for the *expression* of that learning. For instance, how is knowledge acquired from a book, then converted into a verbal communication about what was learned? Are there losses of knowledge along the way in such a process? And are these skills that can be taught? (Bates, 1981, 85)

One point not underlined by Bates is that it is surely significant that the television materials offered the students their only opportunity to apply principles and theories studied elsewhere in real life. Many of those in the sizeable minority that proved unable to do so were probably successful in their study of the correspondence texts. They understood and could converse in written form about the principles and theories mentioned, could satisfy examiners in continuous assessment tests and written papers, yet they could not apply their 'knowledge' to a situation described as 'real-life' or 'real-world'. It would appear that for some students at least the problem of learning how to use the television material may have as much to do with their ability to relate academic understanding to social reality, than with some mysterious psychological set concerned with habitual viewing of television for entertainment.

Two other pieces of evidence may tentatively suggest that inability to 'apply' or relate, often the subject of criticism by businessmen of recent graduates, could be intimately connected with the use of video in open learning. The first has already been mentioned at the beginning of this book. The important work of the Schools Council Project on Communication and Social Skills showed that the creation of audio-visual teaching messages about familiar study material gave numerous children — perhaps especially among those classified as less able — new insight, motivation and expressive ability. If knowledge itself, in the fullest sense, is most fully expressed for some subjects in audio-visual form, translating it into writing may well mean the loss of a great deal of meaning, as Bates hints. Other researchers have certainly suggested something of the sort: 'Cognition in general is viewed as an elaborate audio-visual system . . . our knowledge of the world and of language behaves in some real sense like an elaborate film-library with verbal communications' (Paivio, 1981). If this is so, it is true enough that television (even more so, video) can aid students to develop valuable skills of analysis and application, provided they possess or can acquire the necessary interpretative ability to move easily from one mode of learning to another. In addition, one may surmise that for certain objectives it may be much more effective to utilise the audio-visual medium for study and for assessment much more heavily than has been the convention in education. This has already been suggested in this book in several other contexts and the second piece of evidence re-ferred to above should now be considered.

One of the most frequent uses for video in training in the past has been in simulation. At its most elaborate, in the training of teachers for classroom organisation and discipline, an American development known as microteaching uses video to record brief rehearsed events in a specially prepared classroom, so that a trainee may enact such minor points of method as 'dealing with an interruption' or 'using the black-board to set a task'. After playback, trainee and tutor discuss the event before moving on to a new item or re-enacting the first one with some modification. Most use of video in this area is less carefully structured, but it sometimes offers startling insights. On one occasion a group of postgraduate students on a British university mastership course in Applied Social Studies were enacting a simulated interview between a 'client' (one student) and a 'probation officer' (a second student). As can happen, the two students swiftly identified with their roles and began to play out their interaction with considerable conviction. The 'probation officer' adopted from the outset a somewhat peremptory tone with the 'client' but this expanded into a hostility that clearly took all those watching and (not at the time but on playback) the student herself by surprise. All agreed that the simulated event itself had been a disaster and that the student concerned was clearly in danger of mishandling real-life situations. The most significant fact about this little tale is that the student concerned had achieved first-class honours in her first degree, had a year's 'excellent' achievement in the field to quote and was at the time placed top of her year for her theoretical grasp and ability in written and spoken expression of argument about her subject of study. As the tutor remarked after-wards, 'if for no other reason than to demonstrate to Margaret and to us her inadequacies, the video equipment has today justified its contri-bution to the course'. My own rider to that point would be that Margaret's activities on her course could and should have included both her own analysis of audio-visual material and assessment of simulation exercise work by means of video. Only thus could the gap between abstraction and practice have been bridged effectively.

Video materials therefore seem likely to be especially valuable as open learning opportunities expand. If video is associated for obvious reasons in many adult minds with a mode of entertainment which has absorbed many thousands of hours, if it offers as a study mode not merely illustrative exemplification of argument but the opportunity to analyse and apply theory and principles in real-life situations, it has a particularly important role to play in opening up education to those who have regarded education as a closed book. The word 'book' is significant, too, since for the first time since the sixteenth century we can seriously consider using ways of recording, storing and recalling ideas and knowledge other than by print. Such modes of expression are already being practised by growing numbers of young people in our society. They may also have special value for adults seeking open learning opportunities. In sum, the particular contributions of video to open learning are not only important in themselves, but also offer aid in achieving greater precision in the definition of open learning itself, as we shall see in a moment. Three specific areas of contribution can now be described for video in open learning: these may be called attrac-tion, representation and inspiration.

Attraction

Perhaps the greatest barrier against most citizens taking up open learn-ing opportunities is the initial one. Whereas the small minority in any society that consume and produce most of the creative ideas and know-ledge have no difficulties over seeking out and using the vast bank of information that sustains modern cultures, the majority do not regard the resources as available. Public libraries have been available to most British communities for several generations, yet the majority of those who use them (themselves a minority in society) barely penetrate the topsoil that covers the rich seams of knowledge that more confident and better educated citizens mine. To those who do not use libraries at all, or whose visits consist of repetitive trips to work through the entire works of a small group of romantic fiction authors, or to hover around the 'returned books' area, the idea of education itself has been anathema since they left school. Television, by contrast, is a major source of entertainment, information and persuasion. The attractions of a medium of such variety, pace and colour delivering its messages within one's own home have been manifest for many years now. The development of video offers a gateway to knowledge and ideas such as has never before been available. In North America, where the tradition of adult education has been different from that in Britain, the arrival of a major new broadcast television series is often grasped by local and regional educational agencies, who set up one-day meetings or more extended provision to attract viewers to continue to develop their interest in the subject of the series. If such opportunities were to include suitable video materials for study at home or in, say, a local school or library, the attractive effect of the initial broadcast would stand more chance of survival. This is especially true of citizens who find the conventional modes for distance learning not just unattractive but daunting: the contrast between, say, the experience of viewing 'The Ascent of Man', a lavishly presented exploration of the human achievement in science and technology, and, say, a series of follow-up lectures ('just like school') or reams of printed study materials, however well prepared, can be extreme to the point of pain for a hesitant 'open learner'. Video can be used to sustain the initial interest or indeed to arouse that interest itself, as museums, libraries and art galleries are beginning to discover. The familiarity of the medium, its accessibility, its ability to incorporate an enormous range of presentation forms, and its expressiveness, are all powerful attractors that could be used throughout an open learning scheme to wean students towards other forms of study.

Representation

The implications of video developments for learning . . . are enormous. (ACACE, 1982, 118)

Yet the Report of the Advisory Council on Adult and Continuing Education says little or nothing specific in support of this claim, confining itself (para. 8.33) to pointing out that the immense expansion in the pre-recorded videocassette market implies that these materials will be increasingly utilised in continuing education. There will be little dispute about that. As far as video in open learning (and therefore in continuing education) is concerned, of greater interest and potential significance is the likelihood that presenting a higher proportion of study materials in video form will not only be attractive to students but will also increase the likelihood that unfamiliar information and ideas will be comprehended and used effectively. Combinations of media to represent ideas and clusters of information will become more varied, and it will not be difficult to design open learning opportunities that permit individual students or self-selecting groups to devise alternative routes towards equivalent learning goals. Such developments will in themselves support the motivation of those taking up learning opportunities by giving them greater control over their activities (and a more active role) than in conventional courses.

An imaginable arrangement would run as follows. At the end of a broadcast, a brief announcement attracts a viewer who left school at the age of 14 to write off or telephone for 'further information'. Local libraries and colleges, previously alerted to the likelihood of enquiries, have set up opportunities either to replace existing schemes or in addition to them, and prepared staff to react positively to enquiries. An initial 'learning pack', available either direct from the television or radio station, or local newspaper, library or school (as set out in the 'further information') includes a videocassette that may include a regionally prepared 'starter' to support, encourage, stimulate and maintain the student's first motivation towards learning, as well as material specific to the area of study, or it may be specially prepared to form part of the first study tasks. In either case, the cost of copying from a master videotape onto a cheap cassette or disc is trivial, and the costs of production of the master are roughly comparable to those involved in creating a well-illustrated paperback guide (such as is frequently published in support of a popular broadcast television series). Early essays in this area will have to be subsidised, until, for example, ideas (already standard in Scandinavian countries) about libraries or schools as appropriate sites for individual viewing of video material, even if no machine is available in the student's own, or a friend's, home, become accepted. Within a few years such exercises could become self-sustaining, as students grow used to the idea of paying for these more varied materials, which will retain a resale value after use, and utilising them with confidence. The psychological aspects of representing information in video form, especially for those who lack confidence or who face barriers in more conventional print-based presentations, have already been discussed. From the teaching point of view, as has been pointed out many times in this book, not only are there very few subjects that cannot be treated in video format, but there are some (especially in the practical, 'real-life', area that will be of special interest to a majority of students attracted by open learning opportunities) that are vastly more effective when presented in this form than when written or taught through lecturing.

Inspiration

It may not have been necessary for Isaac Newton to have been struck on the head by an apple, or for Archimedes to put too much water in his tub, for those great minds to have grasped the physical laws with which their names are associated. Yet every child's understanding of the force of gravity and the principle of displacement, is associated with the mythic images of the two philosophers sitting respectively under an apple tree and in a bath. The images have extraordinary force and persistence. In themselves they offer examples of the power of an audio-visual demonstration of an idea, even if most of us have first heard the stories from a teacher or read them in a book. Perhaps more significantly, the stories demonstrate the immense power of the subconscious mind and remind us how many discoveries have been made by accident. One of the results of creating a mixture of study modes, including a portion of video, for open learning packages, rather than relying on print and tuition alone, is to encourage the possibility of minds making similar 'leaps' of inspiration as they consider the course materials they are offered. As has already been noted more than once, the majority of teachers feel most secure teaching by lecture and offering students printed material to study. The reasons are obvious: teacher control is thereby maximised and, of course, thereby the likelihood of dutiful students completing their studies satisfactorily is increased. In the context of open learning, where the student is above all attracted by his or her interest in the subject, rather than a need to achieve an examination credit or a certificate, such control is a barrier to progress and an inhibition to the student's own inspiration. The latter may appear a trivial or immensely rare possibility to those responsible for conventional further education, but is it? Consider that video material can be examined frame by frame, and in fast or slow motion, and that random or computer-guided access to specific frames (or even all those frames in sequence that demonstrate certain characteristics or groups of characteristics, listed by visual or sound cues) is already possible. Later generations of video technology will increase in resources while reducing in price. Such facilities are not just gimmicks or toys. In the context of ideas and knowledge, they offer an awesome potential for discovery and understanding that it is not easy to imagine.

Conclusion: the Future

Professor William Gosling's warning that only the poverty of our own imagination can cheat us of full realisation of the microelectronics promise, has already been quoted. Even now there are those who are working hard to ensure that we do fail to take full advantage of the situation. A report in a British national newspaper in late 1982 hailed the success of the government's microelectronics education programme, aiming to place a micro in every British school. 'Experts predict that within a decade, the micro will be more important in education than conventional methods of study, and far more important than video or overhead projectors.' Since the experts concerned have a personal stake in the success of the micro in education, it would be surprising if they did not see its future as being very important. My own professional role in video ensures that my own view of the importance of video is similarly emphatic. The sinister and damaging aspect of the quotation is the attempt to rank the microcomputer as 'far more important' than video or overhead projectors. This is rather like saying that video will be more important than micros or hand-operated adding machines (which are about as close to microcomputers in power and value as are overhead projectors to video recorders). Worse still, the remark implies an ignorance of the process of convergence to which reference has already been made. The technical forces making microcomputers more and more valuable and less and less expensive are affecting the video industry in like fashion; the educational implications of a shift towards microcomputer-based study are similar to those of by a shift towards video-based study. Within a few years devices will be available that will offer links between the technologies that will have further implications for education and training. It is reasonable to say at this point that it is difficult for us to imagine precisely how such devices will function or what they will imply for learning. It betrays a desperate poverty of imagination to deny that such convergence will occur.

Video, then, has an important part to play in the development of open learning, not only in attracting and retaining students, but in stimulating their fullest outbreaks of intellectual energy. Few would deny that developed countries lacking raw materials (Japan already and others swiftly to follow) and Third World countries lacking the economic advantages of the industrialised societies can hardly afford to overlook the possibility that open learning systems could be used to stimulate and inspire new insights, discoveries and inventions. Open learning may well become not just a vague term to describe an aspect of additional educational provision by the state, but a method of identifying lost talent, new skills and novel solutions to problems of great social and economic import.

From all the above, a clearer definition of open learning itself begins to emerge. Far from being a synonym for distance learning, open learning, with its emphasis on access to existing resources for those who face barriers in conventional educational systems, means the provision of learning opportunities that by definition link to educational and related institutions. Whereas distance learning schemes can conceivably be designed to function for individuals learning throughout on their own, open learning schemes can hardly be designed as such, at least with current technology. Although distance-learning schemes may be 'open' to all, the use of the phrase lays emphasis on the independence and separation of the learner, where 'open learning' implies access to existing facilities, to other learners, and to face-to-face tuition. This in turn implies, once again, that a major obstacle to the development of open learning opportunities lies in the traditions and expectations of colleges and other institutions responsible for further education. As has been remarked above, open learning schemes that attract, retain and inspire students will do so by developing learner-centred materials and courses. This will be seen as undesirable by some who have responsibility for teaching, since it implies a reduction in their control of teaching and learning. On the other hand, it may make it easier to accommodate students whose demands on conventional resources will be less than those of conventional classes. Self-help groups, for example, such as the Scandinavian study-circle system, could be developed, with or without tutors as central figures.

Although the creation of appropriate study materials at first sight appears to be an insuperable problem, the costs as well as the effort required may, in fact, be less serious than appears. Elsewhere in this book it is pointed out that educational video materials will be produced in increasing quantities by broadcasters, commercial agencies and educational institutions. Much of this material will readily and inexpensively adapt into formats appropriate to open learning contexts, and the costs of producing new materials for purposes other than broadcasting are already falling fast. A more significant problem lies in the total inadequacy of current methods of searching for and retrieving passages of video: existing printed catalogues, the only accessible resource, give only titles and brief summaries of a tithe of the constantly growing range of recorded material. One of the most eagerly awaited results of the convergence of video and computer technology must be an ingenious means of entering, cross-referencing and retrieving not just entire films or programmes stored in video form, but passages, even single frames. The videodisc offers a possible means of developing such techniques, without which opening up video to learning may be a slow process.

10 CONTINUING EDUCATION

At the close of that justly celebrated BBC Television series 'The Ascent of Man', the late J. Bronowski laid heavy emphasis on the importance of what he called 'the democracy of the intellect'.

> We must not perish by the distance between people and government, between people and power, by which Babylon and Egypt and Rome failed. And that distance can only be closed if knowledge sits in the homes and heads of ordinary people with no ambition to control others. (Bronowski, 1973, 435)

Continuing education should be seen as a campaign in the war to create a true democracy of the intellect, rather than merely a straightforward continuation of earlier educational or training activities. At the beginning of this book I quoted the psychologist George Kelly and his definition of man as man-the-scientist, an endlessly enquiring figure whose insatiable curiosity is perhaps his most remarkable feature. Although to some 'continuing education' is defined as merely a continuation, a retraining or updating exercise, the phrase in its full power equates with implying both that no one can ever complete their own specialist education and that few, if any, topics are not of some interest to all of us. Socrates would have approved this concept of continuing education, for although he regarded the training of the young in certain skills as essential, he thought no man truly 'wise', least of all himself, and was interested in a great range of topics, practical and theoretical, even if he thought the study of wisdom the highest activity of all.

In this final chapter of the book, the political importance of education will be underlined as firmly as it was for Bronowski, and for much the same reasons. The United Kingdom is clearly one of the most wealthy states in the world, and has only recently declined from a position of outstanding economic power. Yet surveys made in 1980 showed that 51 per cent of the British population had *never* taken part in *any* form of education or training since completing their initial education (CPRS, 1980). The Advisory Council for Adult and Continuing Education in 1982 published a report on continuing education in which it called for a national policy to plan for a comprehensive system aiming to narrow the gap between the well educated and the poorly educated in Britain. The arguments they advanced in support of this view, apply, as they themselves say, to all other countries, too: 'A democratic society can only be sustained by its individual citizens' ability to take part in and contribute to economic, social and cultural change and growth' (ACACE, 1982, 184). Yet since it is generally the well educated who continue to consume educational opportunities, what part, if any, can video in particular play in attracting, retaining and aiding those who have always tended to regard education as not for them at all?

The preceding two chapters have, of course, suggested a number of ways in which video may be expected to play a very significant role in continuing education in the next 20 years. As the Advisory Council itself acknowledges at the end of its Report, the opportunities for new learners depend for their realisation upon changes that the existing institutions begin to make now, not only in their arrangements for adult learning but in their attitudes to learning materials, to equipment and to other institutions. Meanwhile, the Open University is studying the implications of its growing experience with continuing education courses, already mentioned, with their relatively small demands on the learner, very limited barriers (low-level textual 'reading age', computer-marked assignment only) and so forth. A recent study suggests that such materials will always have important secondary usage either for those who purchase them, or for others, or both; that however carefully structured a package may be, the learner may ignore the sequence, recommended method of study and the stated objectives of a course; and that the learner will work at his or her own pace and perhaps even have learning needs that are difficult to predict in advance or to interpret in retrospect (Calder, 1982). This baffling diversity of usage and reaction can be used as ammunition for those who regard provision of such courses as an extravagant experiment on the fringes of education, especially as the secondary usage mentioned suggests serious loss of potential revenue, a revenue that to such critics is probably the sole justification of the provision. On the other hand, the diversity of learning activity may be seen as offering strong evidence that these courses have indeed been attracting, retaining and aiding students averse to conventional adult-education schemes.

A key problem facing the Open University Centre for Continuing Education as well as for others interested in the subject, is underlined by the observations described above. The variety of learning strategies adopted by those following the short courses prepared by the Open University does not of itself imply the paramount glory of the adult learner's skill in resolving problems posed and taking opportunities offered. Many students, even at undergraduate level, appear to have no awareness at all of the way they study, especially if they have never been challenged, either by a self-conscious effort or by the quality of the learning task they face, to think about learning itself. Such students may understand 'knowledge' as 'correct answers' (preferably one answer to each question) and seek to extract such knowledge from whatever materials are placed before them. A more sophisticated stance is to regard a learning task as a form of puzzle, which has to be solved to find the right answers. At a later stage, a student (in any subject) will recognise that it may be possible to think about an issue from several positions, that a particular view may be 'right' or 'wrong' according to context, but that one's assessment of that explanation will depend on a number of criteria which may be utilised in turn or in concert to test it and reach what may always be a tentative judgement. At the same time the approach of an adult learner to a learning task, even more than that of a child, will be influenced by the particular reasons for undertaking it: personal background, expectations for the future, and so on. Still, if it is possible to help students develop increasingly sophisticated perceptions of how they learn and the nature of understanding, to do so is sufficient aim in itself for an entire educational system. 'A goal of the whole of education should be to encourage such development, and this should clearly be the central goal of any direct attempt to improve students learning' (Gibbs, Morgan and Taylor, 1982, 28). The wide availability of television in video format has revolutionary implications for education for two major reasons, both related to the development of understanding in the deepest sense. First, access to ideas and information is immensely enhanced; secondly, our own interpretation and expression of ideas is affected by video.

Access to Ideas and Information: the Role of Video

Access in several senses was a major concern of the earlier chapter on 'Video in Open Learning'. Perceptions of how one learns, mentioned above, also have a great deal to do with access, since they may impose a serious barrier not only to the understanding of an issue but to progress beyond a certain stage in a particular subject and outwards to other subjects. Another recent Open University study discussed the heterogeneity of adult students and how they learn from different media

(Field, 1982). Clear-cut differences are observable in appreciation of the broadcast television components of Open University courses, according to the presumed reason for study. The vocationally oriented student tends to find broadcast television material unhelpful for various reasons, including inability to relate it to other parts of the course, and to work with it at their own pace. The non-vocational student whose main motivation is personal development tends to be much more enthusiastic, finding it stimulating because it 'puts the course in context' and 'shows wider implications'. In the same publication, Field discusses the extremely favourable rating given by Open University students to summer school, the week-long residential study experience already discussed. Despite the problems posed for students by having to arrange for attendance at summer school, a major reason for its success lies in the *access to ideas* offered. Summer schools come second only to course texts for 'giving help in your studies', and Field suggests that the major reason is the discretion students are allowed to order and space the learning opportunities available to them. At a summer school the learning process takes place in a way more similar to the study of course texts than any other medium: ideas can be shared readily, pursued while doing other things (e.g. over a meal), repeated at will, skimmed or studied closely, and so on. 'Whether summer school or text, it helps to have the medium so organised that students can negotiate their way to the educational meaning implicit in the medium' (Field, 125). The significance of video, whether cassette or disc, is that it offers students similar power to negotiate their way to an idea and beyond.

In discussing both open learning and distance education the economic and social realities of late twentieth-century society force one to think and write about access to existing institutions or at least to existing institutional arrangements. Continuing education is a topic that encourages us to look further afield. Some Open University staff have already perceived that the long-term development of continuing education implies that, in addition to the provision of arrangements to satisfy learning needs predicted by an organisation (even when these needs are identified from careful surveys of population and so forth), needs identification itself is coming to be more democratised. Broadcast television, as well as video and personal computer resources, will play a part in this process, of course. However, it is not just a matter of institutions identifying needs more precisely, by asking the customers themselves. In an era when access to ideas and information has become enormously easier, retrieving information or expressing ideas (key objectives in traditional education) are less important than knowing how to gain access to relevant ideas, and how to select and manipulate items or groups of data from the vast banks of information available. In addition,

> the very activity of needs identification, the process itself, is a major learning experience. The adult who examines his circumstances against overt criteria and determines a course of educational action, especially if he does this with a trusted adviser, acquires self-awareness, self-confidence and self-motivation and becomes capable of truly independent learning. (Moore, 1980, 27)

As the home-based learner acquires greater power to achieve access to ideas and information, the significance of the home base itself will be recognised. Richardson (1980) has already argued that even in the 1970s the fact that already 77 per cent of Open University student work time was spent in the home was not properly acknowledged by the institutional approach to study. The microprocessor revolution will tilt the balance for continuing education yet further towards home-based learning. Reference has already been made to interactive video in this context. At the Annual Conference of the Educational Television Association in 1982, delegates attended the first public presentation by the Institute of Educational Technology from the Open University of their pilot system to produce and operate an interactive video system (Laurillard, 1982). Sequences of video are intercut with interactive question and answer programs controlled by an Apple microcomputer. The technology is cumbersome at present, as is the slow process of designing and creating appropriate software. Nevertheless the pilot system is promising enough, like the Sony Video Responder described elsewhere, or any one of several other pilot projects, to demonstrate the enormous potential of computer-controlled audio-visual material. As videodiscs or other devices that can carry much-increased amounts of such material, randomly accessible, individual usage of such a hoard could be guided by appropriately programmed software, to include some elements of interactivity. Different students could use the same (mass-produced) material in individual manner according to need, by means of the specific software developed for them (Roach, 1982b). In the long term, the tedious business of creating software may itself become a simpler process and sophisticated indexing should in any case reduce the need for computer-controlled access to video material.

Interpretation and Expression of Ideas: the Significance of Video

At various points in this book there have been references to the significance for education of expressing ideas in video form rather than in print. Reference has been made to the work of Carol Lorac and Michael Weiss, and we shall return again below to the Schools Council Project in Communication and Social Skills. While this book is not primarily concerned with the academic area known as communication studies, some light can be shed on the subject of the role of video in continuing education by reference to it. 'Communication Studies' is an area of academic interest in which attention has generally been concentrated on the process or processes of communication or else on the text and context of the message. The former approach tends to concentrate on communication in the sense of the transmission of messages, their reception and the stimulation of activity that follows; the latter approach concentrates on communication in the sense of the expression and interpretation of meaning, and the interaction of communicator, text of communication and audience. An excellent new introduction to study of the area makes some attempt to bring the two approaches more closely together (Fiske, 1982). John Fiske regards the semiotic approach to study of communication, concentrating on text, as particularly valuable in helping us understand the significance of the innumerable messages we generate and interpret each day. Yet his own discussion of semiotics and meaning shows how interrelated the psychological, sociological and cultural approaches to the study of communication have become:

> Semiotics sees communication as the generation of meaning in messages — whether by the encoder or the decoder. Meaning is not an absolute, static concept to be found neatly parcelled up in the message. Meaning is an active process . . . the result of a dynamic interaction between sign, interpretant and object. (Fiske, 1982, 49)

Psychiatry would accept (and even extend) this view of communication and of the generation and interpretation of meaning, since it fits well with modern approaches to the study of human behaviour (e.g. Watzlawick *et al.*, 1967).

Modern philosophy also stresses the dynamic nature of communication by emphasising the inadequacy of our attempts to seek truth, which will always ultimately elude us, 'for all is but a woven web of guesses' (Popper, 1963). George Kelly's concept of man as 'man-the-scientist', who views and so construes and reconstrues the world according to his own set of psychological criteria is also relevant. The theory does not only describe human understanding in a manner that accommodates both the power of human reason and the inadequacy of human ability to do more than glimpse reality. It has also generated a useful empirical method — the repertory grid technique — of exploring our perceptions and interpretations of events. The repertory grid has proved particularly useful in the study of the dynamics of television viewing (Baggaley and Duck, 1976). As advertising experts have long known, the rich experience of viewing and hearing a successful television commercial involves receiving and interpreting far more subtle messages than a straightforward imperative to buy a specific product. Of course the subtlety is intended to encourage the subconscious changes of attitude that ensure purchase of one product in preference to a rival. Baggaley and Duck have shown that many of the 'production variables' of television presentation — for example, the way in which a news interview may be shot — have unpredicted but powerful effects on many viewers' perceptions of the relative authority of the interviewee, the relative truthfulness of the report, and so on. The variables extend to such apparently extraneous factors as whether a news presenter is seen with a blank background, or against still or moving images. Such findings are a reminder both of how little we still appreciate of our own understanding of reality, and how powerful is the influence of vision on our perceptions.

It has already been suggested that education has so far failed to reform its methods of teaching to take account of such points. Even before the revolutionary processes discussed in this book were under way, it was true that modern students, through their enormous experience of television, tended to be pictorially highly literate. Education has for generations concentrated on the presentation of ideas in verbal form, involving primarily the left hemisphere of the brain which controls logic as well as verbal and numerical calculation. The right hemisphere of the brain appears to control spatial understanding, manipulative abilities and pictorial imagery. As anyone who has ever used mnemonics to assist in recalling long lists knows, verbal memories (left brain) can be triggered readily and reliably by visual memories (right brain) (Gilder, 1982). In a world where personal memory, an individual's ability to recall data, is of less significance than hitherto, but the ability to select, interpret, manipulate and apply data is paramount, education urgently needs to review its traditional approaches to design of study materials. If the encoding and decoding of ideas in written form becomes even a little less prevalent (and the evidence suggests that effects will be much more marked within 20 years) it is perversity itself to insist that all educational progress shall continue to be measured entirely by the ability to interpret and express ideas in written form. As discussed in the previous chapter, the opportunity to express ideas or information in audio-visual form has been shown to have a catalytic effect for children classified as less able by traditional measures. There is every reason to suppose that the effect will be observed in other parts of the lifespan, when those responsible for continuing education begin to encourage student use of video not only to interpret but to express ideas.

Video in Continuing Education: the Approach to AD 2000

Over the 20 years between 1960 and 1980, the percentage of the EEC workforce employed in service industries grew from 38.4 to 53.4 while those employed in manufacture fell from 36 per cent to 29 per cent over the same period (figures quoted from the *ILO Yearbook of Statistics*). As John Atkin, a vice-president of Citibank, has pointed out, it is already a misnomer to describe the members of the EEC as industrial countries (Atkin, 1982, 17). Nearly half of those employed in the service sector are engaged in tradeable services, those that can be sold abroad. Education and training already form a valuable and growing part of these tradeable services for the EEC, mainly sold to newly industrialised countries as they move from one level of technology to another in the search for new markets. The continued expansion of tradeable services as an area of economic activity and increasing employment will not at first sight have much to offer middle-aged citizens with highly specific manual skills, say, redundant steelworkers, but the tide is ebbing quickly and strongly away from traditional manufacturing industry as the backbone of European economies. Those who ignore the flow will eventually be left stranded. Continuing education has in fact become more significant for the future economic health of the EEC nations than even initial education. Retraining has suddenly acquired major new significance, not only in the sense of being a necessary experience for increasing numbers of citizens, but also in the sense of being an important industry in its own right.

Video has a particularly important part to play in this industry with its vital export potential. There is neither the time, nor the resources, nor the methodology available to create sufficient text-based or computer-based or tutor-centred courses for all the demands being expressed; and indeed text, computer and tutor each on their own, can no longer be imagined as suitable for the task of continuing education and training. Similarly, it would be quixotic to claim that video can be expected to shoulder these new responsibilities alone. The technological convergence between computer and video hardware implies that some of the obstacles that have impeded development work recently are about to be dispelled, but the human problems that still obstruct progress will be more difficult to solve. One of the most promising features to be observed is, of course, the swift growth of the video industry itself, already mentioned in other contexts. A movement towards adaptation of educational approaches can be expected to take place in any case in the next decade, as the social and economic influence of video continues to grow.

What of the Third World? A recent issue of the *Bulletin of the Institute of Development Studies* painted such a gloomy picture of the impact of microelectronics on international trade that the newspaper report of the issue was headed 'The Time-bomb in the Computer' (Kaplinsky, 1982). The IDS argument is that the microelectronics revolution is already having such far-reaching effects on industry in the developed world that even the cheap labour advantage of the Third World is losing its attraction to major investors. It is suggested that although the new technologies can be operated effectively in Third World countries without large numbers of highly skilled staff, back-up services and neighbouring firms using similar systems are rarely available in a developing country. Therefore multi-national companies are now withdrawing investment. The effect is predicted to be economically disastrous. Further, the lack of software production skills in Third World countries is not helped by the fact that little attention has yet been directed to the development of new technology appropriate to a developing country's needs, so that the possibility of indigenous software firms emerging does not seem likely at present. These are serious weaknesses, especially in an era of such very rapid change. Yet it is at least imaginable that (as the article itself implies at one point) key parts of education and training might be reformed in the Third World, to reverse the trend foreseen. The converse is also true: without new education and training approaches the impact of microtechnology on the developing world is likely to be damaging. There is a further point. The IDS argument implies that the only forces available are market forces. In developing countries, however, governments may themselves resolve to invest effort in education and training to support economic changes they wish to develop. For example, higher education in Singapore is planned to grow by 50 per cent in terms of student numbers and investment within the current decade; the Republic of China is spending over 300 million dollars between 1982 and 1985 on developing its education, training and research programmes (Land, 1982). There is at least some prospect that such action may join forces with the economic attraction to the wealthy countries of exporting education, to offer real advances in the agriculture-based economies of Third World nations, perhaps in directions that will not even represent competition with their traditional competitors and economic masters.

The last remark above may sound idealistic, even romantic. Yet the world into which we are emerging is an unfamiliar one. One can already observe one nation leapfrogging another in technological know-how, achieving economic advantage, only to suffer the effects of over-production or the employment by yet another nation of a more advanced technology still. The economic future of the world is unpredictable and unstable, not only because of the insane military arrangements in which we engage, not only because of our ecological destructiveness and apparently uncontrollable population growth, but because the processes of economic development are no longer entirely clear, if they ever were. All that can be said, and it can be stated with emphasis, is that the arguments advanced elsewhere in this book for reforming educational methods, although addressed primarily to Britain and her economic and cultural allies, apply *a fortiori* to the Third World, and therefore world-wide. A conference paper delivered in late 1982 by the Manager of Technology Assessment Services at the National Computing Centre was addressed to those responsible for education in Britain. Every word of Philip Virgo's urgent message can be applied to every nation, North and South, even if some of the contexts and purposes mentioned would have to be adapted to the needs of the specific society.

Having stressed how recently constructed, i.e. only for the past three generations, is the 'traditional' content of British education, by which an academic university-oriented education was imposed on all children, Virgo argues that the enormous challenge to us radically to reorganise education is one that can be met and that must be met swiftly. Comparing the impact of low-cost video to the sixpenny libraries that appeared in every aspiring working-man's household a hundred years ago, he underlines the labour-intensive nature of production of video: each university and polytechnic should be planning large-scale production of video and computer-aided video materials, as the central development of its continuing education programme. In so doing many more jobs and, as Virgo does not observe, many more *projects* attracting fee-paid work, will be created, so that those with creative imagination and technical or craft skills will have new opportunities to take. As might be expected from a speaker who has a clear appreciation of the potential of microtechnology to transform some aspects of work, Virgo suggests that the real challenge to education is far greater than to create computer awareness or computer literacy among young people. For example, since the new technology is particularly appropriate for the performance of instant analyses of data, the interpretation of such analysis should become a primary skill, alongside the three Rs. The ability to simulate, in the sense of running a computer model in reverse to test the conditions necessary for the achievement of a specific result, is the sort of skill that all should acquire, now, at whatever age they may be. Similarly, since self-employment is already becoming a predominant mode of life in Britain, education should offer commercial and business training for *all* in school and (Virgo should have added) throughout life. It seems likely that at least 25 per cent of the British workforce can expect at some stage in their lives to be their own boss: at present, few are ready. Virgo's conclusion is clear and pressing:

Only the widespread use of video packages and computer-based training techniques can enable our teaching workforce to respond in the time available. A redeployment of existing resources . . . to enable the teachers to retrain in-service and learn the new skills by using the new technology . . . is the only option available if one believes that we have, at best, a decade in which to achieve the turnaround. (Virgo, 1982, 7)

AFTERWORD

In re-reading this book, I have become conscious of certain features that surprised me. First, there is an element of repetition, at least in terms of my conclusions on the various issues discussed. To an extent, that feature must bear witness that I am less imaginative than I would like to think: co-operation between individuals and institutions is recommended over and over again; re-consideration of the content as well as the methodology of much education recurs many times; an emphasis on the benefits of learner-centred education can be found in every chapter. Yet, on reflection, I justify the presence of this leitmotive (for it is in fact a single theme) on two grounds. First, these are matters of policy that can be applied, just as their workings can be exemplified, at all levels of education. It would be possible to do so in a single school or as a national policy. Therefore, given the radical nature of the challenge posed in Chapter 1, it is understandable that it has been repeated in the context of each topic discussed. Secondly, repetition is justified, it seems to me, not only because of the applicability of the ideas to all areas of education and training, but because of the significance and urgency of the need to make decisions. This is simply because many of the issues raised have already been the subject of recommendations by far more influential figures than the author for many years now. The economic difficulties of the past decade have combined with our consciousness of the technological and other uncertainties before us, to prevent action. Indeed, as far as government educational policies in Britain, and indeed in many countries, are concerned, the last decade has been marked more by conservative reaction than radical reform.

This is no longer simply a matter of political preference. As Professor Gosling and many other authorities have stressed, certain developments in technology and at least some of their economic effects are quite assured between now and the end of the twentieth century. The choice lying before those with educational responsibility in every society is whether to withhold consent from the implications of the revolutions that are already upon us, or to play a part in affecting their results. In a time of uncertainty there is a great temptation to sit still, to wait out the storm, and indeed there are advantages in such a policy. Would it be wise, on this occasion?

Just as I was completing the manuscript of this book, I attended a meeting organised by the Teaching Methods Committee of a distinguished British university. The subject was the impact on the university of the 'various revolutions that are affecting our work' and how far teaching methods were altering in response. Four senior members of academic staff spoke to the assembled audience of staff and students. Not one referred to any of the issues discussed in this book, although of course they were all aware of a contraction in public spending in Britain which was leading to large numbers of voluntary redundancies at the institution. There is little doubt that universities can continue indefinitely without changing their ways of storing, retrieving and exchanging information and ideas. The result will not be eventual closure, but it will mean contraction, as external forces do become economic and intellectual revolutions. More intriguing than the example of conservatism quoted above was the open discussion that followed the hour of lectures. In it, student after student criticised the dominance of the lecture method, questioned the aims of university education, raised points about the employment of graduates or the narrowness of PhD topics. In every case, one or other of the points raised in this book had a bearing on the discussion; even more significantly, the academics responding to the questions tended to agree that a major purpose, if not the major purpose, of university education was to stimulate ways of thinking, rather than to instil facts. They tended to agree that the explosion of available information and its accessibility meant that rehearsing facts was no longer an appropriate skill in most subjects. They bewailed students' inability or unwillingness to express themselves boldly in tutorials, but acknowledged that there was little stimulus for them to do so.

In other words, there is at least a recognition, an awareness of the problems and choices for educational content and method, even among authorities who do not welcome the prospect of radical change and who hanker for the calmer period of the postwar expansion of economies and educational provision. Indeed, many teachers will the ends, but do not see, or even resist, the means to achieve them. Nevertheless, those who do recognise that reform is necessary should also be able to see that reform is urgent. At the end of a series of powerful articles on the educational revolution and modern society, published in the summer of 1982 in *The Times Higher Education Supplement*, Peter Scott quoted the words in which, 40 years earlier, the historian W.J. Cash summed up the mentality of the American South:

Proud, brave, honourable by its lights, courteous, personally generous, loyal, swift to act, but signally effective, sometimes terrible in its action — such was the South at its best. Violence, intolerance, aversion and suspicion towards new ideas, an incapacity for analysis, an inclination to act from feeling rather than from thought, an exaggerated individualism and a too narrow concept of social responsibility, attachment to fictions and false values . . . sentimentality and a lack of realism — these have been its characteristic vices in the past. And, despite changes for the better, they remain its characteristic vices today.

Scott suggested that these words might be applied to 'post-imperial, post-liberal Britain'. Perhaps so; they also should give pause to educators in Britain and in other countries, who are facing unprecedented challenges today and for the next decade, challenges which will be renewed until they are met.

Those who do meet the challenges of the new technology and welcome video not only as a useful technique to carry existing ideas but as a way of stimulating change in the way we study and teach, and the bases of our understanding of subjects, will find they are swimming with powerful tides beneath and around them. That metaphor is not a soothing one. Swimming with a current is an alarming experience as the stream bears one towards unknown rapids, submerged rocks and an uncertain destination. But it is less tiring than attempting the other direction, and one has a realistic prospect of reaching a landing of one's choice, by calculating when to swim and in which direction, and when to float. There is another point, perhaps the most appropriate on which to end a book about the implications of video for communication and education. There are difficulties besetting all of us like myself who can look back on 20 years as a teacher and who still cherish and instinctively use such old-fashioned devices as books as authorities and tools. Our children, although perfectly capable of using books, do not share our single-minded dependence upon them to generate ideas and information. They move confidently and enthusiastically in the electronic jungle and their abilities are our best hope for the future. Whereas the medieval European tradition of education was that a child should be treated as a small-scale man, with all that that entailed for the authority and wisdom of the full-scale teacher, we have entered an era in which Wordsworth's 'the child is father to the man' has acquired a new potency.

BIBLIOGRAPHY

Abatemarco, F. (1981, 1982a, 1982b) 'New Products and Processes', *Newsweek*, 21 December 1981, 12 July 1982, 19 July 1982

ACACE (The Advisory Council for Adult and Continuing Education) 1982) *Continuing Education: from Politics to Practice*, Leicester: Advisory Council for Adult and Continuing Education

Adler, R.P., Lesser, G.S., Meringoff, L.K., Robertson, T.S., Rossiter, J.R. and Ward, S. (1980) *The Effects of Television Advertising on Children*, Lexington: D.C. Heath

Aikman, A.A. (1982) 'A New Dimension in Teaching Experimental Science', *Journal of Educational Television, 8*, 2, 113-18

Atkin, J. (1982) 'Where the Jobs will be in 2000 AD', *Guardian* (Financial Extra), 15 March 1982, 17

Baggaley, J. and Duck, S. (1976) *Dynamics of Television*, Farnborough: Saxon House

Banks, D.A. (1981) 'Technology, Society and Adult Education', University of Leeds: Dissertation for Diploma in Adult Education

Bannister, D. and Fransella, F. (1971) *Inquiring Man: The Theory of Personal Constructs*, Harmondsworth: Penguin

Bates, A.W. (1978) 'New Technology for Home-based Learning: the Challenge to Campus-based Institutions', *Journal of Educational Television, 4*, 2, 4-13

Bates, A.W. (1981) 'Some Unique Characteristics of Television and some Implications for Teaching and Learning', *Journal of Educational Television, 7*, 3, 79-86

Bates, A.W. (1982) 'The Impact of Educational Radio', *Media in Education and Development, 15*, 3, 144-9

Bates, A.W. and Gallagher, M. (eds.) (1978) *Formative Evaluation of Educational Television Programmes*, London: Council for Educational Technology

Bates, A.W. and Robinson, J. (eds.) (1977) *Evaluating Educational Television and Radio*, Milton Keynes: Open University Press

BBC (1966) *Educational Television and Radio in Britain*, papers prepared for a National Conference in Sussex, London: BBC

BBC (1982) *Insight* (Annual Programme for BBC Continuing Education, 1982-3), London: BBC

Beard, R.M., Bligh, D.A. and Harding, A.G. (1978) *Research into*

Teaching Methods in Higher Education, Guildford: Society for Research into Higher Education

Bligh, D. (1972) *What's the Use of Lectures?* Harmondsworth: Penguin

Bligh, D. (1977) 'Are Teaching Innovations in Post-Secondary Education Irrelevant' in Howe, J.A. (ed.), *Adult Learning: Psychological Research and Applications*, New York: John Wiley

Brew, A. (1978) 'An Open University Course in a Conventional University', *Teaching at a Distance, 12*, 1

Brew, A. (1982) 'The Process of Innovation in University Teaching', *British Journal of Educational Technology, 2*, 13, 153-62

Briggs, A. (1961) *The History of Broadcasting in the United Kingdom, Vol. 1 — The Birth of Broadcasting*, London: Oxford University Press

Bronowski, J. (1973) *The Ascent of Man*, London: BBC

Brooks, R. (1982a) 'Can this Man Switch on Britain?', *The Sunday Times*, 22 March 1982

Brooks, R. (1982b) '30-channel TV gets Thatcher Go-ahead', *The Sunday Times*, 29 August 1982

Brooks, R. (1982c) 'What's on TV now in Milton Keynes?', *The Sunday Times*, 3 October 1982

Brooks, R. and Collie, J. (1982) 'Big Three to Land Sky-high TV Deal', *The Sunday Times*, 28 February 1982

Brown, G. (1978) *Lecturing and Explaining*, London: Methuen

Brown, M. (1982) 'It's one thing to Export Education', *Guardian*, 12 January 1982

Bruner, J.S. (1966) *Towards a Theory of Instruction*, Cambridge, Mass.: Harvard University Press

Brynmor Jones (1965) *Audio-Visual Aids in Higher Scientific Education*, London: HMSO

Cabinet Office (1982) *Cable Systems*, London: HMSO

Calder, J. (1982) 'Adult Learning and Continuing Education', *Teaching at a Distance Institutional Research Review, 1*, 137-56

Carey, P. (1981) 'Telematics: the Impact on Industry', *Journal of the Royal Society of Arts, 5299*, 413-23

CET (Council for Educational Technology) (1979) *The Contribution of Educational Technology to Higher Education in the 1990s*, London: Council of Educational Technology

Carson, I. (1982) 'December Deal for Cable TV', *The Observer*, 25 April 1982

Chittock, J. (1981) 'Goodbye Gutenberg . . . Hallo Hollywood!', *Sight and Sound*, 164-9

154 *Bibliography*

Coldevin, G.O. (1979) 'Broadcasting Development and Research in Tanzania', *Journal of Educational Television, 5*, 3, 70-5

Coldevin, G.O. (1980) 'Broadcasting Development and Research in Kenya', *Journal of Educational Television, 6*, 2, 61-7

Connors, B. (1979) 'An Introduction to Self-Instruction' in Rowntree and Connors (1979), 10-83 (q.v.)

CPRS (Central Policy Review Staff) (1980) *Education, Training and Industrial Performance*, London: HMSO

Dainton, F. (1979) 'Do we get the Universities we Deserve?', *University of Leeds Review, 22*, 32-52

Dallos, R. (1980) 'Active Learning and Television', *Teaching at a Distance, 17*, 39-44

Daniel, J.S. (1975) 'Learning Styles and Strategies: the Work of Gordon Pask' in Entwistle and Hounsell (eds.) (1975), 83-92 (q.v.)

Daniel, J.S. and Marquis, C. (1977) 'Interaction and Independence', reprinted in *Teaching at a Distance, 14* (1979), 29-44

Department of Education and Science (1973) *Adult Education: a Plan for Development* (The Russell Report), London: HMSO

Department of Education and Science/Scottish Education Department (1978) *Higher Education into the 1990s* (The Oakes Report), London: DES

Dunn, G. (1977) *The Box in the Corner: Television and the Under-Fives*, London: Macmillan

Dunn, G. (1980) 'Television and the Education of the Young', *Journal of Educational Television, 6*, 2, 47-52

Durbridge, N. (1981) 'The Adult Learner and E.t.v.', *Educational Broadcasting International, 14*, 2, 82-4

Entwistle, N. and Hounsell, D. (eds.) (1975) *How Students Learn*, Lancaster: University of Lancaster

Fiddick, P. (1982) 'Rescuing Cable Television from its Shameful Beginnings', *Guardian*, 18 October 1982

Field, J. (1982) 'Student Learning from Media: Student Diversity versus the Centralised Institution', *Teaching at a Distance Institutional Research Review, 1*, 101-35

Fielden, J. and Pearson, P.K. (1978) *Costing Educational Practice*, London: Council for Educational Technology

Fiske, J. (1982) *Introduction to Communication Studies*, London: Methuen

Francis, S. (1982) 'Cable's First Five', *Broadcast*, 29 March 1982, 28-33

Freeman, R. (1976) 'Open Learning Now?', *The Listener*, 14 October 1976

Freeman, R. (1979) 'Botanic Man: Education or Entertainment', *Teaching at a Distance, 16,* 19-23

Freeman, R. (1982) 'Reflections on an Open Tech', *Teaching at a Distance, 21,* 6-9

Freire, P. (1968) *Pedagogy of the Oppressed,* Harmondsworth: Penguin

Frons, M. and Willenson, K. (1982) 'Japan's Bell Labs', *Newsweek,* 9 August 1982, 30

Gibbs, G., Morgan, A. and Taylor, E. (1982) 'Why Students Don't Learn', *Teaching at a Distance Institutional Research Review, 1,* 9-32

Gilder, R.S. (1982) 'Left Brain – Right Brain Theory and the Design of Medical Teaching Materials', *Journal of Audiovisual Media in Medicine, 5,* 45-50

Giles, K. (1979) Review of J.A. Howe (ed.) (1977) *Adult Learning* in *Teaching at a Distance, 14,* 77-80

Giles, K. and Allman, P. (1981) 'The Cognitive Development of Adults', *Teaching at a Distance, 20,* 29-35

Glynn, L. and Hewitt, W. (1982) 'The Telematics Shake-up', *Newsweek,* 25 January 1982, 40

Gosling, W. (1978) *Microcircuits, Society and Education* (Occasional Paper 8), London: Council for Educational Technology

Gosling, W. (1980) 'Three Steps to a Revolution', *Journal of Educational Television, 6,* 3

Groombridge, B. (1972) *Television and the People,* Harmondsworth: Penguin

Halsey, A.H., Heath, A.F. and Ridge, J.M. (1980) *Origins and Destinations: Family, Class and Education in Modern Britain,* Oxford: Clarendon Press

Hart, I. (1982) 'Educational Television: the Gulf between Researchers and Producers', *Journal of Educational Television, 8,* 2, 91-8

Hartley, J. and Cameron, A. (1967) 'Some Observations on the Efficiency of Lecturing', *Educational Review, 20,* 1, 30-7

Hartley, J. and Davies, I.K. (1978) 'Note-taking: A Critical Review', *Programmed Learning and Educational Technology, 15,* 207-24

Hayter, C.G. (1974) *Using Broadcasts in Schools,* London: BBC/ITA

Hopson, B. and Scally, M. (1980) *Lifeskills Teaching,* London: McGraw Hill

Horlock, J. (1982) 'Updating the Professional', *Media in Education and Development, 15,* 1, 7-8

Howe, J.A. (ed.) (1977) *Adult Learning: Psychological Research and Applications,* New York: John Wiley

Howkins, J. (1982) 'Broadcasting in the Age of Information Technology', *Television*, March/April 1982, 3-5

Jenkins, C. and Sherman, B. (1979) *The Collapse of Work*, London:
Eyre Methuen

Jolly, B. (1981) 'Videotaped Case Histories in the Final MB (Psychiatry)
Examination at St. Bartholomew's Hospital Medical College', *Journal
of Audiovisual Media in Medicine, 4*, 123-6

Kaplinsky, R. (1982) 'The Time-bomb in the Computer', *Guardian*, 21
May 1982

Katz, E. and Wedell, G. (1978) *Broadcasting in the Third World –
Promise and Performance*, London: Macmillan

Kelly, G.A. (1955) *The Psychology of Personal Constructs*, New York:
Norton

Kelly, G.A. (1964) 'The Language of Hypothesis', *Journal of Individual
Psychology, 20*, 137-52

Kirk, D. (1982a) 'The Video Disc is Dead', *Video, 8*, 5 (March) 3

Kirk, D. (1982b) 'The Software Bubble', *Video, 8*, 8 (July), 3

Kleinman, P. (1982) 'Watch and Wipe Magazine', *Guardian*, 19 August
1982

Land, T. (1982) 'China Invests in Western Technology', *The Times
Higher Education Supplement*, 30 April 1982

Large, P. (1982) 'Cutprice Computer Power from the Space of Two
Attache Cases', *Guardian*, 24 August 1982

Laurillard, D.M. (1979) 'The Process of Student Learning', *Higher
Education, 8*, 4, 395-409

Laurillard, D.M. (1982) 'The Potential of Interactive Video', *Journal
of Educational Television, 8*, 3, 173-80

Lewell, J. (1981) 'Computers Extend the Artist's Horizon', *New
Scientist*, 10 December 1982, 750-4

Lloyd-Kolkin, D. (1981) 'Marketing Educational Programmes to
Commercial Broadcasters', *Journal of Educational Television, 7*, 3,
90-2

Lloyd-Kolkin, D. (1982) 'Teaching Students to Become Critical Television Viewers', *Journal of Educational Television, 8*, 2, 99-108

Lorac, C. and Weiss, M. (1981) *Communication and Social Skills*,
Exeter: Wheaton

Lowe, S. (1982a) 'The Technology of Satellite Broadcasting', *Video,
8*, 5 (March) 22-6

Lowe, S. (1982b) 'The Economics of Satellite Broadcasting', *Video, 8*,
6 (April), 16-19

McIntosh, N. (1976) *A Degree of Difference*, Guildford: Society for

Research into Higher Education

Mackenzie, N., Postgate, R. and Scupham, J. (1975) *Open Learning – Systems and Problems in Post Secondary Education*, Paris: UNESCO

McRae, H. (1982) 'When it Comes to TV Viewing, Staring at Words or Figures Takes a Back Seat', *Guardian*, 25 August 1982

Maddison, J. (1980) *National Education and the Microelectronics Revolution*, Clevedon: Clevedon Press

Manpower Services Commission (1982) *Open Tech Task Group Report*, London: Manpower Services Commission

Marbach, W.D. *et al*. (1982a), 'To each his own Computer', *Newsweek*, 22 February 1982, 40-6

Marbach, W.D., Sandza, R. and Doi, A. (1982b) 'Computers in a Briefcase', *Newsweek*, 30 August 1982, 43

Matthews, A. (1978) *Trade Union Studies: A Partnership in Adult Education*, London: BBC

Media Project (1982a) *Channel Four and Social Action Broadcasting – A Symposium*, Berkhamsted: Volunteer Centre Media Project

Media Project (1982b) *Directory of Social Action Programmes*, Berkhamsted: Volunteer Centre Media Project

Moberly, W. (1949) *The Crisis in the University*, London: Student Christian Movement Press

Moore, M. (1980) 'Continuing Education and the Assessment of Learner Needs', *Teaching at a Distance, 17*, 26-9

Moss, G.D. (1979) 'The Influence of Open University Distance Teaching in Higher Education', *Teaching at a Distance, 14*, 14-18

Moss, J.R. (1976) 'The Teacher and the Producer', *University Vision, 14*, March, 33-40

Moss, J.R. (1979) 'Mystery, Mastery and Open Minds', *University of Leeds Review, 22*, 138-51, Leeds: University of Leeds

Murray, J.F. (1981) *The Future of Educational Broadcasting – a Discussion Paper*, Glasgow: Scottish Council for Educational Technology

Muslin, H.L., Thumblad, R.J., Templeton, B. *et al*. (1974) *Evaluative Methods in Psychiatric Education*, Washington: American Psychiatric Association

Nielsen, Co., A.C. (1979) *The Television Audience*, Chicago: A.C. Nielsen

Noble, G. (1975) *Children in Front of the Small Screen*, London: Constable

O'Grady, C. (1980) Report on Schools Television, *The Times Educational Supplement*, 26 September 1980

Owen, D. and Dunton, M. (1982) *The Complete Handbook of Video*,

Harmondsworth: Penguin

Paffard, M.G. (1973) *Inglorious Wordsworths*, London: Hodder and Stoughton

Paivio, A. (1981) 'Imagery as a Private Audio-Visual Aid', *Instructional Science, 9*, 4, 295-309

Peters, F.J.J. (1981) 'An Electronic Academic Journal', *Journal of Educational Television, 7*, 3

Popper, K. (1963) *Conjectures and Refutations: the Growth of Scientific Knowledge*, London: Routledge and Kegan Paul

Ramsey, D. and Willenson, K. (1982) 'A Superbrain Search', *Newsweek*, 9 August 1982, 34

Richardson, M. (1980) 'The Home-Based Learner in the 1980s and 1990s', *Teaching at a Distance, 17*, 19-25

Roach, D.K. (1980) 'Has Educational Television Arrived?', *Journal of Educational Television, 6*, 3, 74-7

Roach, D.K. (1982a) Editorial in *Journal of Educational Television, 8*, 2, 87-90

Roach, D.K. (1982b) 'Media in Education' (editorial), *Journal of Educational Television, 8*, 3, 170-2

Rogers, C. (1969) *Freedom to Learn*, Columbus, Ohio: Merrill

Rogers, J. (1977) *Adults Learning* (2nd edn), Milton Keynes: Open University Press

Rowley, C. (1981) 'An Overview of Television in the U.S.A. and Some Implications for Britain', IBA: unpublished

Rowntree, D. and Connors, B. (eds.) (1979) *How to Develop Self-Instructional Teaching*, Milton Keynes: Open University Press

Rutter, M. (1979) *Fifteen Thousand Hours*, London: Open Books

Scally, M. and Hopson, B. (1981) *Lifeskills Teaching in Schools and Colleges* (mimeo), Leeds: Counselling and Career Development Unit, University of Leeds

Scott, P. (1982) 'Towards a Post-Binary Future', *The Times Higher Education Supplement*, 27 August 1982

Scupham, J. (1967) *Broadcasting and the Community*, London: C.A. Watts

Skinner, B.F. (1954) 'The Science of Learning and the Art of Teaching', *Harvard Educational Review, 24*, 88-97

Spencer, D.C. (1980) *Thinking About Open Learning Systems* (Working Paper 19), London: Council for Educational Technology

Starks, R. (1982) 'Consequences of Cable Deregulation for Broadcasting', *Television*, July/August 1982, 9-10

Stephen, K.D. (1982) 'New Trends at the Tertiary Level', *Media in*

Education and Development, 15, 1, 3-6

Stringer, R. (1982) 'Video Companies Prefer Doing it Themselves', *Daily Telegraph*, 25 January 1982

Super, D.E. and Bowlesbey, J.A. (1979) *Guided Career Exploration*, New York: Psychological Corporation

Tarpy, R.M. (1975) *Basic Principles of Learning*, Boulder: Scott, Foresman

Tomlinson, J.R.G. (1981) 'Education in the Eighties', *Journal of the Royal Society of Arts, 5303*, October 1981, 725-33

Turner, B.M. and Mackenzie, A. (1982) 'Interactive Software', *Television*, May/June, 5-7

Turney, J. (1982) 'The Magazine on the Screen', *The Times Higher Education Supplement*, 27 August 1982

Unwin, R. (1980) 'Visual Shock', *The Times Educational Supplement*, 5 December 1980

Virgo, P. (1982) 'New Work for Old', *Guardian*, 26 October 1982

Walters, B. (1981) 'Electronic Meetings – U.S.A. Leads', *Conferences and Exhibitions International*, October, 32

Waniewicz, I. (1981) 'The TV Ontario Academy: the Use of Television Broadcasting and Computer-managed Learning for Adults', *Educational Broadcasting International, 14*, 2, 78-81

Ware, E. (1982) 'Social Agencies and Channel Four' in *Media Project* 1982a), 9 (q.v.)

Watzlawick, P., Helmick Beavin, J. and Jackson, D.D. (1967) *Pragmatics of Human Communication*, New York: Norton

Wels, I. (1982) 'A Dish Full of Channels', *Broadcast*, 25 January 1982

Wenham, B. (1982) 'Third Age of Broadcasting', *Observer*, 21 March 1982

Williams, R. (1971) *The Long Revolution*, Harmondsworth: Penguin

Williams, R. (ed.) (1981) *Contact: Human Communication and Its History*, London: Thames and Hudson

Willis, N. (1981) 'The Tele Becomes the Tool', *Journal of Educational Television, 7*, 3, 97-9

Yeomans, K. (1982) 'Adult Education and Broadcasting', *Media in Education and Development, 15*, 3, 142-4

Yorke, D.M. (1981) *Patterns of Teaching*, London: Council for Educational Technology

Young, E.C. (1979) (ed.) *New Penguin Dictionary of Electronics*, Harmondsworth: Penguin

Young, M., Perraton, H., Jenkins, J. and Dodds, T. (1980) *Distance Teaching for the Third World (The Lion and the Clockwork Mouse)*, London: Routledge and Kegan Paul

INDEX